Thriving Through Turbulence

Arun Kumar

Published by Arun Kumar, 2024.

THRIVING THROUGH TURBULENCE

First edition. January 13, 2024.

ISBN: 979-8224477678

Written by Arun Kumar.

Dedication

The information provided in this book, "Thriving Through Turbulence," is for educational and informational purposes only. The content is intended to assist readers in understanding various aspects of navigating economic downturns and should not be considered as financial advice.

The author and publisher are not licensed financial advisors, and the content within this book does not constitute personalized financial, investment, or legal advice. Every individual's financial situation is unique, and readers are encouraged to consult with qualified professionals, such as financial advisors, tax consultants, or legal experts, before making any financial decisions.

The strategies, concepts, and examples presented in this book are based on historical data and general market observations. Past performance is not indicative of future results, and investment outcomes can vary based on individual circumstances, market conditions, and other factors.

Readers are reminded that investing always involves risk, and it is important to conduct thorough research and analysis before making any investment decisions. The author and publisher disclaim any liability for financial losses or damages resulting from the use of the information presented in this book.

Ultimately, readers are responsible for their own financial decisions, and this book serves as a guide for educational purposes. It is recommended to seek professional advice tailored to individual circumstances to make informed and appropriate financial choices.

Chapter 1: Introduction - Navigating Turbulent Times

In the unpredictable landscape of economic cycles, navigating through turbulent times requires a unique set of skills, knowledge, and a resilient mindset. This introductory chapter sets the stage for understanding the intricacies of investing during recessions, offering a roadmap for readers to not only survive but thrive in the face of economic downturns.

Setting the Stage for Investing During Recessions

The Symphony of Economic Peaks and Valleys

The financial markets, akin to the ebb and flow of tides, experience periods of prosperity and decline. Recessions, often feared and misunderstood, are an inherent part of this cyclical dance. In "Thriving Through Turbulence," we embark on a journey to demystify the complexities surrounding economic downturns, shedding light on opportunities that lie within the shadows.

Shifting Perspectives: Challenges as Catalysts

Rather than viewing recessions as insurmountable obstacles, we'll explore the concept of adversity as a catalyst for growth. History has shown that some of the most successful investors and entrepreneurs have emerged not despite but because of economic challenges. By understanding the patterns and nuances of recessions, we can uncover hidden potential and transform uncertainty into strategic advantage.

The Evolution of Investment Philosophy

To thrive through turbulence, one must embrace a dynamic and evolving investment philosophy. We'll discuss how traditional notions of investing may need to adapt in the face of economic uncertainties. As we navigate the intricate web of financial markets, we'll uncover the importance of agility, foresight, and a proactive approach to investment.

Building a Foundation of Knowledge

In this chapter, we lay the groundwork for the journey ahead, delving into the fundamentals of recessions, their historical context, and the broader economic landscape. By understanding the forces at play, readers will be better equipped to make informed decisions, transforming challenges into opportunities for financial growth.

Nurturing a Resilient Mindset

Beyond the technical aspects of investing, emotional resilience stands as a cornerstone for success. We'll explore strategies to manage the inevitable emotional rollercoaster that accompanies market fluctuations. Learning to navigate the peaks and valleys of investment with composure can be the differentiator between weathering the storm and flourishing in its wake.

Your Guide Through Uncharted Waters

As we embark on this expedition through economic downturns, remember that this book serves not only as a guide but as a companion in your journey toward financial resilience. Each chapter unfolds a new facet of the turbulent terrain, offering insights, strategies, and real-life examples to illuminate the path forward.

In the chapters to come, we will delve deeper into the mechanics of recessions, explore alternative investments, dissect market behaviors, and glean wisdom from seasoned investors. Together, we will not only confront the challenges presented by economic downturns but also uncover the opportunities that lie beneath the surface.

• • • •

A PRELUDE TO OPPORTUNITY

Embracing Uncertainty as a Constant

In the realm of investing, uncertainty is the only constant. As we navigate through the uncharted waters of economic downturns, the ability to adapt becomes paramount. We'll explore how embracing the inherent unpredictability of financial markets can empower investors to turn challenges into stepping stones towards prosperity.

The Ripple Effect: Understanding Recessions

Before we delve into the strategies and insights, let's first unravel the essence of recessions. Chapter 2 will provide a comprehensive understanding of what recessions are and how they reverberate through the economic landscape. By comprehending the root causes and signals of downturns, investors can position themselves strategically to ride the waves of economic change.

Lessons from the Past: Illuminating the Path Forward

Chapter 3 invites readers on a historical journey through significant recessions, dissecting pivotal moments such as the 2008 financial crisis and the dot-com crash. These historical narratives serve as invaluable guides, offering insights into the patterns, pitfalls, and triumphs of those who have navigated economic storms before us.

Digital Assets: A Modern Beacon in Downturns

In Chapter 4, we'll explore a contemporary dimension of investing – the role of digital assets. From digital art to cryptocurrencies, these alternative investments have emerged as intriguing options during economic challenges. By understanding the potential of digital assets, readers will be equipped to diversify their portfolios in an ever-evolving financial landscape.

The Dance of Markets: Behavior During Recessions

Chapter 5 invites us to observe the intricate dance of financial markets during recessions. By analyzing historical market behaviors, we can discern patterns, identify opportunities, and anticipate potential pitfalls. Armed with this knowledge, investors can navigate the tumultuous seas with a compass of informed decision-making.

Riding the Rollercoaster: Emotional Resilience in Investing

Investing is not merely a numbers game; it is a psychological challenge. Chapter 6 addresses the emotional rollercoaster that often accompanies market fluctuations. Through proven strategies and psychological insights, readers will learn to maintain composure, make rational decisions, and avoid the pitfalls of panic-driven actions.

Proactive Approaches: Investment Strategies During Recessions

Chapter 7 lays out a strategic playbook, detailing proactive approaches for investors to weather economic storms. From defensive investment strategies to seizing unique opportunities, this chapter provides a toolkit for readers to navigate through downturns with confidence and foresight.

Risk Mitigation: Safeguarding Your Investments

In Chapter 8, we delve into the crucial aspect of risk management. By highlighting effective risk mitigation strategies, readers will be empowered to protect their investments and navigate economic downturns with a greater sense of security.

Real-Life Triumphs: Case Studies of Successful Investments

Chapter 9 offers a closer look at real-life success stories during recessions. By examining thriving investments, readers gain insights into the practical applications of strategies discussed throughout the book. These case studies serve as beacons of inspiration, illuminating the path to financial resilience.

A Preview of What Lies Ahead

As we embark on this journey together, remember that thriving through turbulence is not just a destination but a continuous process of adaptation, learning, and growth. In the subsequent chapters, we will explore post-recession opportunities, gather insights from seasoned investors, and culminate our expedition in the concluding chapter with key takeaways to guide you in thriving through uncertain times.

Unveiling the Aftermath: Preparing for Post-Recession Opportunities

In Chapter 10, "Preparing for the Aftermath," we shift our focus towards the horizon that follows economic downturns. This chapter serves as a strategic guide for readers to position themselves for the opportunities that often arise in the aftermath of recessions. By exploring post-recession dynamics, we lay the groundwork for building a resilient portfolio that not only weathers storms but also thrives in the calm that follows.

The Phoenix Rises: Opportunities Amidst the Ashes

As economies recover and rebuild, astute investors can uncover unique opportunities for growth. We will delve into sectors and industries that historically have experienced rebounds, providing insights into where potential future successes may lie. Understanding these trends enables investors to position themselves strategically, ready to capitalize on emerging prospects.

Strategic Reinvestment: Navigating the Recovery

Recession recovery is not a one-size-fits-all process. Chapter 10 will guide readers on how to strategically reinvest during the recovery phase, seizing opportunities that align with their risk tolerance and financial goals. From undervalued assets to emerging markets, we will explore avenues for reinvestment that align with a proactive and adaptive investment philosophy.

Wisdom from the Wise: Expert Insights

In Chapter 11, we turn to the voices of experience. Seasoned investors and financial experts share their perspectives, providing invaluable insights into navigating economic downturns. By gathering wisdom from those who have weathered multiple storms, readers can benefit from the collective knowledge of individuals who have successfully steered their portfolios through challenging times.

Lessons Learned: A Tapestry of Perspectives

As we navigate through the diverse insights of experts, readers will discover a tapestry of perspectives that enriches their understanding of thriving through turbulence. From risk management strategies to unconventional investment approaches, this chapter acts as a forum for learning from those who have honed their skills in the crucible of economic uncertainties.

The Finale: Chapter 12 - Conclusion - Thriving in Uncertain Times

In our concluding chapter, we bring together the threads of wisdom woven throughout "Thriving Through Turbulence." Here, we summarize key takeaways, distilling the essence of navigating economic downturns into actionable insights. Readers will find encouragement, guidance, and a roadmap for not only surviving but truly thriving in the ever-changing landscape of financial markets.

Resilience Redefined: A New Paradigm of Investing

As we bid farewell to the pages of this book, the journey towards financial resilience continues. Chapter 12 serves as a beacon, inspiring readers to redefine resilience as an ongoing process of adaptation and growth. By embracing the lessons learned and forging ahead with newfound knowledge, readers are poised to navigate the future with confidence and resilience.

Your Personal Roadmap: Charting the Course Ahead

In the concluding chapter, readers will find a practical guide for applying the principles discussed throughout the book to their unique financial circumstances. This personalized roadmap empowers individuals to chart a course that aligns with their goals, risk tolerance, and vision for financial prosperity.

A Call to Action: Thriving Through Turbulence Together

As the final pages turn, consider this not just a conclusion but a call to action. "Thriving Through Turbulence" is more than a book; it is a companion on your journey towards financial well-being. May the insights gained within these chapters serve as the wind in your sails, propelling you towards a future where economic challenges are not roadblocks but stepping stones towards financial success.

So, dear reader, as you close the cover of "Thriving Through Turbulence," remember that the journey towards financial resilience is ongoing. May you thrive in uncertain times and navigate the ever-changing tides of the financial world with confidence, knowledge, and unwavering resilience.

Chapter 2: Understanding Recessions

Section 1: Defining Recessions

The Economic Ebb and Flow

In the opening section, we delve into the very nature of recessions, defining them as periods of economic decline characterized by a decrease in economic activity. By exploring key indicators such as GDP contraction, rising unemployment, and diminishing consumer spending, readers will gain a nuanced understanding of the complex mechanisms that signal the onset of a recession.

The Role of Central Banks

Understanding the role of central banks in managing economic cycles is paramount. We unravel the intricate dance between monetary policy, interest rates, and their impact on economic stability. Through clear and accessible language, readers will grasp the tools wielded by central banks to navigate the economic landscape and mitigate the severity of recessions.

Section 2: Causes and Triggers

Unveiling the Catalysts

This section dissects the various triggers that set the stage for a recession. From financial imbalances to external shocks, readers will gain insight into the multifaceted factors that contribute to economic downturns. Case studies and historical examples illuminate how recessions often result from a confluence of events, creating a comprehensive view of the complex forces at play.

The Domino Effect: Global Interconnectedness

In an era of globalized economies, understanding the interconnectedness of nations is essential. This subsection explores how events in one part of the world can trigger a ripple effect, impacting economies far beyond the epicenter. Real-world examples, including the 2008 financial crisis, showcase the domino effect and emphasize the importance of a global perspective in recession analysis.

Section 3: Phases of a Recession

From Boom to Bust

A recession is not a singular event but a process with distinct phases. This section delineates the stages of a typical recessionary cycle, from the initial shock to the eventual recovery. By examining each phase in detail, readers will gain a comprehensive understanding of how economic landscapes transform during these tumultuous times.

The Anatomy of a Downturn

Building on the phases, this subsection delves into the specifics of economic decline. From shrinking business investments to the impact on consumer behavior, readers will explore the intricate details of a recession's anatomy. Graphs, charts, and real-world examples enhance comprehension, providing a visual narrative of the economic shifts that occur during downturns.

Section 4: Societal Impact

Beyond the Balance Sheet

This section transcends economic indicators to explore the human dimension of recessions. By examining the societal impact, we delve into the consequences for individuals, families, and communities. Unemployment rates, social inequalities, and the psychological toll of economic uncertainty become focal points, adding depth to readers' comprehension of the far-reaching effects of recessions.

Case Studies: Human Stories Amidst Economic Challenges

Embedded within this subsection are case studies that illuminate the real-life stories of individuals and communities navigating recessions. Personal narratives provide a poignant and relatable dimension to the economic concepts discussed, fostering empathy and emphasizing the tangible, human consequences of economic downturns.

Section 5: Looking Ahead

Navigating the Uncertain Future

As we conclude Chapter 2, the focus shifts towards the future. We explore the challenges and opportunities presented by the unpredictable nature of recessions. By considering emerging trends and potential scenarios, readers are equipped to anticipate economic shifts and make informed decisions in the chapters that follow.

The Constant Evolution: Adapting to Economic Realities

The closing subsection emphasizes the dynamic nature of economic landscapes. By acknowledging the evolving nature of recessions, readers are encouraged to adopt a mindset of adaptability and continuous learning. This forward-looking perspective sets the stage for the proactive approaches and strategies detailed in subsequent chapters.

Section 6: Global Perspectives on Recessions

Macro and Microeconomic Factors

Diving further into the understanding of recessions, this subsection explores both macro and microeconomic factors that contribute to economic contractions. Readers will explore the role of government policies, international trade dynamics, and the impact of technological advancements. By distinguishing between broader economic trends and industry-specific influences, readers can develop a nuanced comprehension of the diverse forces shaping recessions.

Comparative Analysis: Historical Recession Patterns

To deepen the understanding of recessions, this section conducts a comparative analysis of historical recession patterns. By examining the similarities and differences between various downturns, readers gain insights into recurrent themes and unique characteristics. This historical context acts as a valuable tool for anticipating future economic shifts and making informed investment decisions.

Section 7: Financial Markets and Recessions

Interplay Between Markets and Economic Downturns

This section unravels the intricate relationship between financial markets and recessions. Readers will explore how market sentiments, investor behavior, and financial instruments respond to economic contractions. Case studies of past recessions provide a real-world perspective on how markets can both amplify and mitigate the impacts of economic downturns.

The Behavioral Economics of Recessions

Delving into the realm of behavioral economics, this subsection investigates how human psychology influences market dynamics during recessions. From herd mentality to cognitive biases, readers will gain insights into the emotional underpinnings of market fluctuations. Understanding these psychological aspects equips investors with the knowledge needed to navigate the markets with a rational and strategic mindset.

Section 8: Government Intervention and Economic Stimulus

The Role of Fiscal and Monetary Policies

This section sheds light on the role of government intervention in mitigating the effects of recessions. Readers will explore the tools available to governments, including fiscal policies (such as stimulus packages) and monetary policies (such as interest rate adjustments). Through case studies, readers will witness the impact of government interventions on recession outcomes.

The Trade-Offs: Balancing Economic Stability

While government interventions can provide crucial support during recessions, there are inherent trade-offs and challenges. This subsection examines the delicate balance governments must strike between stimulating economic activity and avoiding long-term negative consequences. Readers will gain an appreciation for the complexities involved in crafting effective policies to navigate economic downturns.

Section 9: Leading Indicators and Early Warning Signs

Anticipating the Storm: Key Indicators

This section equips readers with the tools to anticipate economic downturns by exploring leading indicators and early warning signs.

From analyzing unemployment rates to scrutinizing manufacturing data, readers will learn to decipher signals that precede recessions. This proactive approach empowers investors to make timely adjustments to their portfolios, potentially mitigating the impact of economic contractions.

The Art of Forecasting: Economic Predictions

Building on the concept of leading indicators, this subsection delves into the art and science of economic forecasting. Readers will gain insights into how economists and financial analysts use various models and data points to predict economic trends. By understanding the nuances of forecasting, readers can critically evaluate predictions and incorporate them into their investment strategies.

Section 10: The Globalization Paradox

The Double-Edged Sword of Globalization

This section explores the paradoxical nature of globalization in the context of recessions. While interconnected economies can amplify the speed and intensity of economic contractions, they also offer avenues for diversification and resilience. Through case studies and real-world examples, readers will navigate the complexities of the globalization paradox and its implications for investors.

Navigating Risk and Reward in a Globalized World

The closing subsection encourages readers to reflect on the risks and rewards associated with a globalized economy. By weighing the benefits of international diversification against the challenges posed by global economic interdependence, readers can make informed decisions that align with their risk tolerance and investment objectives.

Section 11: Recessions and Industry Dynamics

Sectoral Vulnerabilities

This section delves into the nuanced impact of recessions on different industries. Not all sectors are affected equally, and understanding the vulnerabilities and strengths of various industries is crucial for investors. Case studies and analysis provide insight into why certain sectors may thrive during economic downturns while others face significant challenges.

Innovation Amidst Adversity

Building on the industry-specific impact, this subsection explores the role of innovation during recessions. Historical examples illustrate how economic downturns often catalyze technological advancements and business innovation. Readers will gain an appreciation for the resilience of industries that leverage adversity to drive transformative change and emerge stronger on the other side.

Section 12: Behavioral Economics in Recessions

The Emotional Landscape of Investors

This section takes a closer look at the emotional dynamics of investors during recessions. Drawing on principles of behavioral economics, readers will explore common emotional responses, from fear and panic to opportunism and resilience. Recognizing these emotional patterns is essential for developing strategies to navigate the market's psychological ebbs and flows.

Cognitive Biases and Decision-Making

In a deeper exploration of behavioral economics, this subsection dissects cognitive biases that can influence decision-making during economic downturns. Confirmation bias, loss aversion, and herd mentality are among the cognitive pitfalls discussed. Practical insights and strategies are provided to help readers mitigate the impact of these biases on their investment decisions.

Section 13: Environmental, Social, and Governance (ESG) Factors

The Rise of Sustainable Investing

This section examines the growing relevance of Environmental, Social, and Governance (ESG) factors in investment decisions, even amidst economic downturns. Readers will gain insights into how companies' environmental and social practices, as well as their governance structures, can impact long-term investment viability. Case studies highlight instances where ESG considerations have played a pivotal role in navigating economic challenges.

Ethical Investing in Turbulent Times

Building on ESG considerations, this subsection explores the intersection of ethics and investing during recessions. Readers are encouraged to reflect on how ethical principles can guide investment choices, even in the midst of economic uncertainty. By aligning investments with personal values, individuals can navigate turbulent times with a sense of purpose and social responsibility.

Section 14: Recessions and Technological Transformations

Acceleration of Digital Trends

This section investigates the role of technological transformations during recessions, particularly the acceleration of digital trends. Case studies illustrate how technology-driven industries have not only weathered economic downturns but have also thrived by adapting to changing consumer behaviors. Readers gain insights into the opportunities presented by the digital landscape, even in challenging economic climates.

Investing in the Digital Future

Building on the technological theme, this subsection provides practical guidance on investing in the digital future during recessions. From fintech to artificial intelligence, readers will explore sectors that may offer growth opportunities amidst economic challenges. Strategic considerations and risk management principles are presented to guide investors in navigating the evolving digital landscape.

Section 15: Preparing for Economic Resilience

Building a Resilient Portfolio

As Chapter 2 concludes, readers are guided towards building a resilient portfolio that can withstand the challenges posed by recessions. Practical tips, diversification strategies, and risk management techniques are provided to help readers fortify their investment portfolios. The emphasis is on creating a well-balanced and adaptable financial strategy that aligns with individual goals and risk tolerance.

The Role of Continuous Learning

The closing subsection reinforces the importance of continuous learning in navigating economic uncertainties. In a rapidly changing financial landscape, staying informed and adapting to new information is key. Readers are encouraged to view education as an ongoing process, empowering them to thrive through turbulence by staying ahead of market dynamics and evolving economic trends.

Section 16: The Global Economic Landscape

Trade Dynamics and Recessions

This section unveils the intricacies of global trade dynamics and their profound impact on economic downturns. Readers will explore how disruptions in international trade can both trigger and exacerbate recessions. Case studies and historical examples shed light on the delicate balance between globalization and economic stability, providing insights into the interconnected nature of the global economy.

Currency Markets: A Window into Global Sentiment

Delving into the realm of currency markets, this subsection explores how shifts in global sentiment are reflected in exchange rates. Readers will gain an understanding of how currency markets serve as a barometer for investor confidence and geopolitical stability during recessions. Practical insights into navigating currency risks and opportunities are provided to equip readers for the global economic landscape.

Section 17: Technological Disruptions and Economic Shifts

The Fourth Industrial Revolution

This section examines the profound influence of technological disruptions on economic shifts during recessions. From the advent of artificial intelligence to advancements in automation, readers will explore how the Fourth Industrial Revolution is reshaping industries and employment landscapes. Real-world examples illustrate how technological innovations can drive economic transformations even in the face of downturns.

The Human Element: Adapting to Technological Change

Building on technological disruptions, this subsection focuses on the human element of adapting to technological change. Readers will gain insights into the skills and mindsets that are crucial for navigating the evolving job market. Strategies for continuous learning, upskilling, and staying agile in the face of technological advancements are presented to empower individuals during economic uncertainties.

Section 18: Government Debt and Fiscal Policy

The Balancing Act of Fiscal Policy

This section explores the delicate balance governments must strike when implementing fiscal policies during recessions. Readers will gain insights into the implications of accumulating government debt as a means of stimulating economic activity. Case studies and historical perspectives provide a nuanced understanding of the trade-offs and challenges associated with expansive fiscal measures.

Inflation and Deflation: Economic Indicators

Delving into economic indicators, this subsection dissects the impact of inflation and deflation on recessions. Readers will explore how these forces influence consumer behavior, interest rates, and overall economic stability. Practical insights into adjusting investment strategies based on inflationary or deflationary environments are provided, enhancing readers' ability to navigate diverse economic scenarios.

Section 19: The Role of Psychology in Economic Cycles

Behavioral Economics Revisited

Building on previous discussions of behavioral economics, this section revisits the role of psychology in economic cycles. Readers will explore how collective perceptions and sentiments can influence market trends and economic outcomes. Understanding the psychological underpinnings of economic cycles equips readers to navigate the markets with a heightened awareness of the human factor in financial decision-making.

Investor Sentiment and Market Trends

This subsection delves into the nuances of investor sentiment and its impact on market trends. Through case studies and real-world examples, readers will gain insights into how shifts in investor sentiment can shape market dynamics. Practical strategies for interpreting and responding to investor sentiment are presented, empowering readers to make informed investment decisions.

Section 20: Economic Indicators and Big Data Analytics

Harnessing Big Data for Economic Insights

This section explores the intersection of economic indicators and big data analytics. Readers will gain an understanding of how vast datasets and sophisticated analytics tools can provide real-time insights into economic trends. Case studies showcase instances where big data analytics have been instrumental in predicting and responding to economic shifts, offering readers a glimpse into the future of economic analysis.

The Evolving Landscape of Economic Indicators

Building on the concept of economic indicators, this subsection emphasizes the evolving landscape of these key metrics. Readers will explore emerging indicators that are gaining prominence in the digital age. Insights into deciphering and leveraging these indicators for informed decision-making provide readers with a competitive edge in navigating the complex economic landscape.

Section 21: The Intersection of Politics and Economics

Geopolitical Risks and Economic Resilience

This section examines the intersection of politics and economics, focusing on how geopolitical risks can impact economic resilience. Readers will gain insights into navigating the uncertainties posed by geopolitical events, from trade tensions to international conflicts.

Strategies for managing geopolitical risks within investment portfolios are presented to help readers build a robust and adaptable financial strategy.

Policy Uncertainty and Market Volatility

Building on geopolitical considerations, this subsection explores the impact of policy uncertainty on market volatility. Readers will delve into how shifts in government policies can create market fluctuations and influence investor behavior. Case studies highlight instances where policy uncertainty has shaped market trends, offering practical insights into navigating investment decisions amidst political and policy-related uncertainties.

Section 22: Economic Recovery Strategies

Post-Recession Opportunities

This section shifts the focus towards economic recovery strategies, outlining potential opportunities that arise as economies rebound. Readers will explore sectors and industries that historically experience growth during recovery phases. Case studies and success stories provide inspiration and insights into positioning investment portfolios for post-recession prosperity.

Innovation and Entrepreneurship in Recovery

Building on the theme of recovery, this subsection explores the role of innovation and entrepreneurship in driving economic resurgence. Readers will gain insights into how creative solutions, new business models, and technological advancements can catalyze growth during recovery periods. Practical considerations for investors looking to capitalize on innovation-driven opportunities are presented to guide strategic decision-making.

Section 23: Preparing for the Next Economic Cycle

The Cyclical Nature of Economies

This section underscores the cyclical nature of economies and the inevitability of economic cycles. Readers will gain a holistic perspective on how economic expansions and contractions are interconnected, forming part of the broader economic cycle. Insights into preparing for the next economic cycle, including risk management strategies and portfolio adjustments, empower readers to navigate the perpetual ebb and flow of economic trends.

Long-Term Financial Planning

Building on the theme of preparation, this subsection emphasizes the importance of long-term financial planning in navigating economic cycles. Readers will explore strategies for building resilient portfolios that align with their financial goals and risk tolerance. Practical considerations for crafting a financial plan that withstands the test of time provide readers with a roadmap for enduring and thriving through the ever-evolving economic landscape.

In this extended exploration of Chapter 2, readers have delved into a diverse array of economic concepts, global dynamics, technological transformations, psychological influences, and recovery strategies. Armed with this comprehensive understanding, readers are well-prepared to traverse the remaining chapters of "Thriving Through Turbulence," where they will encounter expert insights, real-life case studies, and actionable strategies for navigating and prospering in uncertain economic times.

Chapter 3: Learning from the Past - The Early 1990s Recession

Section 1: Unraveling the Economic Tapestry

A Symphony of Challenges

The early 1990s recession serves as a poignant example of an economic downturn shaped by a convergence of factors. The savings and loan crisis, characterized by the collapse of numerous savings and loan associations, created a ripple effect throughout the financial sector. High-interest rates implemented to combat inflation added to the strain, exacerbating the economic challenges. A slowdown in consumer spending further fueled the downturn, creating a complex economic tapestry.

The Savings and Loan Crisis: A Catalyst for Economic Turmoil

The chapter begins with an exploration of the savings and loan crisis, examining its origins and the cascading impact on financial institutions. Through case studies and historical analyses, readers gain insights into how mismanagement, risky lending practices, and inadequate government oversight contributed to the crisis. The lessons from this period underscore the importance of prudent financial regulation and the need for institutions to operate within sustainable boundaries.

Section 2: High-Interest Rates and Economic Strain

The Conundrum of Monetary Policy

This section delves into the role of high-interest rates as a tool to combat inflation during the early 1990s. Readers will explore the consequences of monetary policies aimed at taming inflation, particularly their impact on borrowing, investment, and economic growth. Historical context and expert perspectives shed light on the delicate balance policymakers must strike when implementing such measures and the lessons for investors during periods of tight monetary policy.

Navigating Financial Waters: Managing Debt in High-Interest Environments

Building on the discussion of high-interest rates, this subsection provides practical guidance on managing personal finances during periods of economic strain. Readers will gain insights into strategies for mitigating the impact of high-interest rates on debt, from refinancing to prudent budgeting. The experiences of individuals and businesses during the early 1990s recession offer valuable lessons for navigating similar financial challenges in the present.

Section 3: Consumer Spending Slowdown

The Engine of the Economy: Consumer Behavior

This section explores the slowdown in consumer spending as a significant contributor to the early 1990s recession. By examining the factors that led to reduced consumer confidence and spending, readers gain insights into the cyclical nature of consumer behavior during economic downturns. Case studies and market analyses provide a lens through which readers can understand the broader implications for businesses and investors.

Personal Finance Strategies: Adapting to Consumer Spending Trends

Building on the understanding of consumer spending dynamics, this subsection offers practical strategies for individuals to adapt their personal finances during periods of reduced consumer activity. From reevaluating spending habits to identifying investment opportunities in resilient sectors, readers will gain actionable insights into thriving amid economic challenges. The lessons from the early 1990s recession underscore the importance of financial agility in the face of changing consumer landscapes.

Section 4: Lessons for Today - Applying Historical Wisdom

Financial Resilience: An Evergreen Principle

This section synthesizes the lessons from the early 1990s recession and applies them to contemporary financial landscapes. Readers will discover how principles of financial resilience, prudent regulation, and adaptable investment strategies remain relevant across different economic eras. Insights from financial experts and successful investors provide a guide for applying historical wisdom to navigate the uncertainties of today's economic environment.

Regulatory Vigilance: Safeguarding Against Financial Crises

Building on the lessons from the savings and loan crisis, this subsection emphasizes the importance of regulatory vigilance in preventing and mitigating financial crises. Readers will explore how regulatory frameworks have evolved since the early 1990s and gain an understanding of their role in promoting financial stability. Practical considerations for individuals and policymakers alike underscore the ongoing need for vigilant oversight.

Section 5: Strategies for Success - Applying Historical Insights

Diversification and Risk Management: Pillars of Financial Success

This section provides practical strategies for individuals and investors to enhance financial success based on the lessons from the early 1990s recession. Diversification and risk management principles take center stage, offering a roadmap for building resilient portfolios. Real-life examples of successful investors who navigated the challenges of the early 1990s recession serve as inspiration for contemporary financial planning.

Seizing Opportunities Amidst Challenges

Building on the theme of success strategies, this subsection encourages readers to identify opportunities within challenges. By examining how innovative businesses and forward-thinking investors capitalized on the changing economic landscape during the early 1990s recession, readers gain insights into the mindset and strategies that lead to success in dynamic and uncertain times.

Section 6: Navigating Economic Downturns with Confidence

Adaptive Investing: A Framework for Success

The concluding section synthesizes the chapter's insights into a framework for navigating economic downturns with confidence. Readers will discover how adaptive investing, informed by historical wisdom, regulatory awareness, and strategic risk management, can position individuals for success. The chapter closes with a call to action, urging readers to apply the lessons from the early 1990s recession to build resilient and prosperous financial futures.

The Dot-Com Bubble Burst (2000-2001)

Section 1: The Rise and Fall of the Dot-Com Era

The Dot-Com Frenzy

The chapter opens with a vivid exploration of the Dot-Com Bubble, a period marked by unprecedented enthusiasm for internet-based companies in the late 1990s. Investors rushed to capitalize on the potential of the burgeoning digital landscape, resulting in soaring stock prices and a proliferation of new ventures. However, beneath the surface of this euphoria, a bubble was forming, leading to a sharp correction that reverberated through the early 2000s.

Bursting Bubbles: A Prelude to Recession

This section dissects the factors that contributed to the inflation of the Dot-Com Bubble, from speculative investments to overvalued technology stocks. The subsequent bursting of this bubble had far-reaching consequences, triggering a recession characterized by a significant decline in the stock market and the collapse of numerous internet-based companies. The chapter sets the stage by unraveling the dynamics that culminated in one of the most notable economic downturns of the early 21st century.

Section 2: The Dot-Com Fallout: Stock Market Turmoil

Market Correction and Investor Panic

This section delves into the aftermath of the Dot-Com Bubble Burst, examining the stock market turmoil that ensued. Readers will gain insights into how overvalued tech stocks rapidly lost value, causing panic among investors. Case studies and historical analyses provide a lens through which readers can understand the cascading impact of the market correction and the lessons for navigating volatile market conditions.

Risk and Reward: A Closer Look at Investment Strategies

Building on the discussion of market turmoil, this subsection offers practical insights into investment strategies during periods of heightened risk. Readers will explore how the Dot-Com Bubble Burst exposed the dangers of speculative investing and the importance of a diversified portfolio. Real-life examples of investors who weathered the storm by adopting sound investment principles serve as a guide for contemporary financial decision-making.

Section 3: The Dot-Com Fallout: Collapse of Internet-Based Companies

Vanishing Ventures

This section scrutinizes the collapse of numerous internet-based companies in the wake of the Dot-Com Bubble Burst. Readers will gain insights into the factors that led to the demise of once high-flying startups, from unsustainable business models to excessive reliance on venture capital. The experiences of companies that weathered the storm and those that succumbed offer valuable lessons for entrepreneurs and investors alike.

Business Sustainability: A Pillar of Long-Term Success

Building on the discussion of business collapses, this subsection provides practical guidance on building sustainable ventures. Readers will explore how the Dot-Com fallout emphasized the importance of sound business fundamentals, customer-centric strategies, and prudent financial management. Case studies of companies that successfully adapted to changing market conditions offer a roadmap for contemporary entrepreneurs seeking enduring success.

Section 4: Lessons for Today - Applying Historical Wisdom

Prudent Valuation: A Guard Against Speculation

This section synthesizes the lessons from the Dot-Com Bubble Burst and applies them to contemporary financial landscapes. Readers will discover how prudent valuation practices act as a guard against speculative excesses, promoting a more realistic assessment of investment opportunities. Insights from financial experts and successful investors provide a guide for applying historical wisdom to navigate the uncertainties of today's economic environment.

Due Diligence and Informed Investing

Building on the theme of financial wisdom, this subsection emphasizes the importance of due diligence and informed investing. Readers will explore how thoroughly researching investment opportunities, understanding market dynamics, and critically evaluating business models can lead to more informed and strategic investment decisions. Real-life examples highlight the benefits of diligence in mitigating risks and identifying long-term value.

Section 5: Strategies for Success - Applying Historical Insights

Agility and Adaptability: Navigating Technological Shifts

This section provides practical strategies for individuals and investors to enhance financial success based on the lessons from the Dot-Com Bubble Burst. Agility and adaptability take center stage, offering a roadmap for responding to technological shifts and market uncertainties. Real-life examples of successful investors who navigated the challenges of the early 2000s serve as inspiration for contemporary financial planning.

Innovation with Prudence: Navigating Business Landscapes

Building on the theme of success strategies, this subsection encourages readers to embrace innovation with prudence in navigating business landscapes. By examining how successful companies leveraged technological advancements without succumbing to speculative excess, readers gain insights into the mindset and strategies that lead to success in dynamic and uncertain times.

Section 6: Navigating Economic Downturns with Confidence

Adaptable Investing: A Framework for Success

The concluding section synthesizes the chapter's insights into a framework for navigating economic downturns with confidence. Readers will discover how adaptable investing, informed by historical wisdom, prudent valuation, and strategic diligence, can position individuals for success. The chapter closes with a call to action, urging readers to apply the lessons from the Dot-Com Bubble Burst to build resilient and prosperous financial futures.

The Global Financial Crisis (2007-2009)

Section 1: The Unraveling Housing Bubble

Origins of the Crisis

The chapter opens by unraveling the intricate web of factors that led to the Global Financial Crisis (GFC), with a focal point on the collapse of the housing bubble in the United States. Readers will delve into the dynamics of subprime mortgage lending, complex financial instruments, and regulatory oversights that collectively contributed to the build-up of financial vulnerabilities. Understanding the roots of the crisis sets the stage for dissecting its profound impact.

The Domino Effect: Global Economic Downturn

This section explores how the collapse of the housing bubble set off a domino effect, triggering a severe worldwide economic downturn. The interconnectedness of global financial markets and the ripple effects across industries and nations are examined. Case studies and real-world examples illuminate the multifaceted nature of the crisis and its far-reaching consequences.

Section 2: Financial Institutions in Crisis

The Lehman Brothers Collapse

This section delves into the pivotal moment of the Global Financial Crisis—the collapse of Lehman Brothers. Readers will gain insights into the events leading to the demise of one of the largest investment banks and the subsequent shockwaves felt throughout the global financial system. The chapter examines the role of other financial institutions in the crisis and the unprecedented government interventions that followed.

The Fragility of Financial Systems: Risk Management Lessons

Building on the discussion of financial institutions, this subsection explores risk management lessons derived from the GFC. Readers will understand how inadequate risk assessment, overreliance on complex financial instruments, and a lack of transparency contributed to the vulnerability of financial systems. Practical insights into bolstering risk management strategies offer contemporary relevance for individuals and financial institutions alike.

Section 3: The Impact on Main Street: Unemployment and Recession

Economic Contraction and Unemployment

This section examines how the financial crisis translated into real-world impact, causing a severe economic contraction and surging unemployment rates. Readers will gain insights into how businesses struggled, consumers faced financial hardships, and the global economy entered a prolonged recession. Case studies shed light on the human stories amidst economic challenges.

Navigating Personal Finances in Times of Recession

Building on the discussion of the recession's impact, this subsection provides practical guidance on managing personal finances during economic downturns. Readers will explore strategies for navigating unemployment, preserving financial stability, and making informed decisions amid economic uncertainty. The experiences of individuals who successfully weathered the storm serve as a source of inspiration for contemporary financial planning.

Section 4: Government Intervention and Policy Responses

Unprecedented Interventions

This section explores the unprecedented government interventions and policy responses deployed to stabilize financial markets and spur economic recovery. Readers will gain insights into fiscal stimulus measures, monetary policy adjustments, and regulatory reforms implemented to address the systemic risks exposed by the GFC. The chapter analyzes the effectiveness of these interventions and their implications for future economic resilience.

The Role of Government Safeguards: Lessons in Economic Stabilization

Building on the discussion of government interventions, this subsection emphasizes the ongoing importance of government safeguards in maintaining economic stability. Readers will explore how regulatory frameworks, prudent fiscal policies, and coordinated international efforts contribute to safeguarding against future financial crises. Practical considerations for individuals navigating an evolving regulatory landscape offer insights into aligning personal financial strategies with broader economic trends.

Section 5: Lessons for Today - Applying Historical Wisdom

Prudent Borrowing and Lending Practices

This section synthesizes lessons from the GFC and applies them to contemporary financial landscapes. Readers will discover how prudent borrowing and lending practices act as a safeguard against excessive risk-taking and unsustainable debt. Insights from financial experts and successful investors provide a guide for applying historical wisdom to navigate the uncertainties of today's economic environment.

Building Resilient Portfolios: Diversification and Asset Allocation

Building on the theme of financial wisdom, this subsection emphasizes the importance of building resilient portfolios through diversification and strategic asset allocation. Readers will explore how the GFC underscored the risks of concentrated investments and the benefits of a well-balanced, diversified approach. Real-life examples highlight the value of thoughtful portfolio construction in mitigating risks and enhancing long-term financial success.

Section 6: Strategies for Success - Applying Historical Insights

Financial Preparedness: An Essential Mindset

This section provides practical strategies for individuals and investors to enhance financial success based on the lessons from the GFC. Financial preparedness takes center stage, offering a roadmap for building emergency funds, managing debt responsibly, and adopting a proactive mindset in the face of economic uncertainties. Real-life examples of individuals who successfully navigated the challenges of the GFC serve as inspiration for contemporary financial planning.

Entrepreneurial Resilience: Navigating Business Challenges

Building on the theme of success strategies, this subsection encourages readers to embrace entrepreneurial resilience in navigating business challenges. By examining how successful companies adapted their business models and strategies during the GFC, readers gain insights into the mindset and actions that lead to success in dynamic and uncertain times.

Section 7: Navigating Economic Downturns with Confidence

Adaptive Financial Planning: A Framework for Success

The concluding section synthesizes the chapter's insights into a framework for navigating economic downturns with confidence. Readers will discover how adaptive financial planning, informed by historical wisdom, prudent risk management, and strategic preparedness, can position individuals for success. The chapter closes with a call to action, urging readers to apply the lessons from the Global Financial Crisis to build resilient and prosperous financial futures.

The Eurozone Crisis (2009-2013)

Section 1: Unraveling Sovereign Debt Issues

Origins of the Crisis

The chapter commences by unraveling the complex origins of the Eurozone Crisis, focusing on sovereign debt issues that plagued countries like Greece, Portugal, Ireland, Italy, and Spain (commonly referred to as the PIIGS nations). Readers will delve into the interconnected challenges of high levels of public debt, fiscal imbalances, and banking failures. Understanding the roots of the crisis sets the stage for dissecting its profound impact.

Contagion and Financial Market Turmoil

This section explores how sovereign debt issues in some Eurozone countries triggered a domino effect, leading to financial market turmoil and heightened economic uncertainty across the region. The chapter examines how interconnectedness within the Eurozone magnified the impact of individual countries' economic challenges. Real-world examples and case studies shed light on the cascading consequences of the crisis.

Section 2: Banking Failures and Economic Contraction

Strain on Financial Institutions

This section delves into the banking failures that ensued as a consequence of the Eurozone Crisis. Readers will gain insights into how the interconnectedness between sovereign debt and banking sectors intensified the economic challenges faced by the affected nations. The chapter examines the impact on financial institutions, highlighting the fragility of banking systems and the need for comprehensive reforms.

Austerity Measures and Economic Contraction

Building on the discussion of banking failures, this subsection explores the adoption of austerity measures as a response to the crisis. Readers will explore the economic consequences of austerity, including reduced government spending, tax increases, and social impacts. The experiences of countries implementing austerity measures offer valuable lessons for individuals and policymakers navigating economic challenges.

Section 3: Social Impacts and Political Strain

Unemployment and Social Struggles

This section examines the social impacts of the Eurozone Crisis, particularly the surge in unemployment rates and the strain on social systems. Readers will gain insights into how economic contraction and austerity measures led to widespread job losses and social struggles. Real-life stories and case studies illustrate the human toll of the crisis and the challenges faced by individuals and families.

Political Challenges and Policy Responses

Building on the discussion of social impacts, this subsection explores the political challenges faced by governments in the Eurozone. Readers will explore how the crisis strained political systems, led to changes in leadership, and influenced policy responses. The chapter analyzes the effectiveness of various policy measures and the lessons for governments in fostering economic resilience.

Section 4: Lessons for Today - Applying Historical Wisdom

Prudent Fiscal Management

This section synthesizes lessons from the Eurozone Crisis and applies them to contemporary financial landscapes. Readers will discover how prudent fiscal management, including responsible public finances and avoiding excessive debt accumulation, acts as a safeguard against sovereign debt issues. Insights from financial experts and successful policymakers provide a guide for applying historical wisdom to navigate the uncertainties of today's economic environment.

Sustainable Banking Practices

Building on the theme of financial wisdom, this subsection emphasizes the importance of sustainable banking practices. Readers will explore how the Eurozone Crisis underscored the need for robust banking systems, effective regulatory oversight, and prudent risk management. Real-life examples highlight the value of sound banking practices in fostering economic stability and resilience.

Section 5: Strategies for Success - Applying Historical Insights

Personal Financial Resilience: Emergency Funds and Debt Management

This section provides practical strategies for individuals to enhance financial success based on the lessons from the Eurozone Crisis. Personal financial resilience takes center stage, offering a roadmap for building emergency funds, managing debt responsibly, and navigating economic uncertainties. Real-life examples of individuals who successfully weathered the challenges of the crisis serve as inspiration for contemporary financial planning.

Entrepreneurial Adaptability: Navigating Economic Shifts

Building on the theme of success strategies, this subsection encourages readers to embrace entrepreneurial adaptability in navigating economic shifts. By examining how successful businesses adapted to the challenges of the Eurozone Crisis, readers gain insights into the mindset and strategies that lead to success in dynamic and uncertain times.

Section 6: Navigating Economic Downturns with Confidence

Collaborative Economic Policies: A Framework for Success

The concluding section synthesizes the chapter's insights into a framework for navigating economic downturns with confidence. Readers will discover how collaborative economic policies, informed by historical wisdom, prudent fiscal management, and personal financial resilience, can position individuals and nations for success. The chapter closes with a call to action, urging readers to apply the lessons from the Eurozone Crisis to build resilient and prosperous financial futures.

The Great Depression (1929-1939)

Section 1: The Precipice of Economic Despair

The Roaring Twenties and the Stock Market Crash

The chapter unfolds against the backdrop of the vibrant Roaring Twenties, a period marked by economic exuberance and cultural dynamism. It delves into the circumstances leading to the infamous stock market crash of 1929, a watershed moment that triggered the onset of the Great Depression. Readers will explore the euphoria of the preceding decade and the abrupt descent into economic despair, setting the stage for the most severe worldwide economic downturn of the 20th century.

Global Impact: From Boom to Bust

This section unravels the global impact of the Great Depression, transcending national borders and affecting economies around the world. The chapter examines how the collapse of financial markets, a sharp decline in industrial production, and soaring unemployment created a perfect storm of economic devastation. Real-world examples and historical narratives illustrate the profound and lasting consequences of this tumultuous period.

Section 2: Unemployment, Poverty, and Social Turmoil

Breadlines and Hoovervilles

This section delves into the human face of the Great Depression, exploring the unprecedented levels of unemployment, poverty, and social turmoil that defined the era. Readers will gain insights into the stark realities of breadlines, Hoovervilles, and the struggle for survival faced by individuals and families. Real-life stories illuminate the challenges and resilience of those who lived through this unparalleled economic downturn.

The Dust Bowl: Environmental and Economic Catastrophe

Building on the discussion of social turmoil, this subsection examines the environmental catastrophe of the Dust Bowl, which compounded the economic hardships of the Great Depression. Readers will explore how severe drought, coupled with poor agricultural practices, led to widespread crop failures and forced migration. The chapter analyzes the intertwined challenges of economic and environmental crises and the lessons for sustainable economic and environmental stewardship.

Section 3: Government Responses and Policy Shifts

The New Deal: A Paradigm Shift in Economic Policy

This section explores the policy responses to the Great Depression, with a focus on Franklin D. Roosevelt's New Deal. Readers will gain insights into the unprecedented government interventions aimed at stimulating economic recovery, providing relief to the unemployed, and implementing financial reforms. The chapter examines the effectiveness of these policies and their implications for modern economic governance.

Monetary Policy and the Gold Standard

Building on the discussion of government responses, this subsection delves into monetary policy and the abandonment of the gold standard during the Great Depression. Readers will explore how changes in monetary policy, currency devaluation, and the departure from the gold standard influenced economic dynamics. The chapter analyzes the complex relationship between monetary policy and economic stability, offering insights into the contemporary role of central banking.

Section 4: Lessons for Today - Applying Historical Wisdom

Fiscal Stimulus and Counter-Cyclical Policies

This section synthesizes lessons from the Great Depression and applies them to contemporary financial landscapes. Readers will discover how fiscal stimulus and counter-cyclical policies act as powerful tools for mitigating economic downturns. Insights from economic historians and policymakers provide a guide for applying historical wisdom to navigate the uncertainties of today's economic environment.

Social Safety Nets and the Importance of Welfare Programs

Building on the theme of financial wisdom, this subsection emphasizes the importance of social safety nets and welfare programs. Readers will explore how the Great Depression highlighted the need for a robust social support system, offering lessons for contemporary society. Real-life examples showcase the value of welfare programs in fostering economic resilience and reducing inequality.

Section 5: Strategies for Success - Applying Historical Insights

Personal Financial Prudence: Savings and Emergency Planning

This section provides practical strategies for individuals to enhance financial success based on the lessons from the Great Depression.

Personal financial prudence takes center stage, offering a roadmap for building savings, practicing emergency planning, and navigating economic uncertainties. Real-life examples of individuals who successfully weathered the challenges of the era serve as inspiration for contemporary financial planning.

Entrepreneurial Innovation: Navigating Economic Transformations

Building on the theme of success strategies, this subsection encourages readers to embrace entrepreneurial innovation in navigating economic transformations. By examining how successful businesses adapted to the challenges of the Great Depression, readers gain insights into the mindset and strategies that lead to success in dynamic and uncertain times.

Section 6: Navigating Economic Downturns with Confidence

Civic Engagement and Community Resilience: A Framework for Success

The concluding section synthesizes the chapter's insights into a framework for navigating economic downturns with confidence. Readers will discover how civic engagement, community resilience, and individual financial prudence, informed by historical wisdom, can collectively position society for success. The chapter closes with a call to action, urging readers to apply the lessons from the Great Depression to build resilient and prosperous financial futures.

The Post-World War II Recession (1945-1946)

Section 1: Transitioning from Wartime to Peacetime

The War's Economic Legacy

The chapter opens by exploring the economic landscape at the conclusion of World War II, marked by the triumph of Allied forces and the significant transformations in wartime production. Readers will delve into the unique challenges of transitioning from a wartime economy, where production was geared towards military needs, to a peacetime economy with a focus on rebuilding and readjustment.

Demobilization and Economic Realities

This section examines the process of demobilization, as millions of soldiers returned home, war industries scaled back, and wartime contracts came to an end. The chapter sheds light on the economic realities of this transition, including the challenges of absorbing returning veterans into the workforce and shifting production from wartime necessities to consumer goods.

Section 2: The Short-Lived Recession

Economic Contraction and Government Intervention

This section delves into the short-lived recession that occurred in the immediate aftermath of World War II. Readers will explore the factors contributing to the economic contraction, including the temporary slowdown in government spending, as war-related expenditures decreased. The chapter analyzes the role of government intervention in stabilizing the economy during this brief downturn.

The GI Bill and Economic Revival

Building on the discussion of government intervention, this subsection highlights the positive impact of policies such as the GI Bill. Readers will gain insights into how the GI Bill, designed to support returning veterans with education, housing, and employment benefits, played a crucial role in economic revival. The chapter examines the lasting legacy of such policies in shaping post-war prosperity.

Section 3: Employment Shifts and Industrial Adaptation

Employment Challenges and Labor Dynamics

This section explores the employment shifts and labor dynamics during the post-war period. Readers will gain insights into the challenges of reintegrating veterans into the civilian workforce and the changing dynamics of industrial employment. Real-life stories and case studies illuminate the experiences of individuals and industries adapting to the peacetime economy.

Industrial Adaptation and Innovation

Building on the discussion of employment shifts, this subsection examines how industries adapted to the new economic realities. Readers will explore the innovations and adaptations that fueled post-war industrial growth, from technological advancements to shifts in production focus. The chapter analyzes the entrepreneurial spirit that emerged during this period and its relevance to contemporary economic transformations.

Section 4: Lessons for Today - Applying Historical Wisdom

Economic Resilience through Adaptability

This section synthesizes lessons from the Post-World War II Recession and applies them to contemporary financial landscapes. Readers will discover how economic resilience through adaptability became a cornerstone of post-war recovery. Insights from historical experiences provide a guide for individuals and businesses in navigating economic shifts and uncertainties.

Government Policies as Catalysts for Economic Recovery

Building on the theme of financial wisdom, this subsection emphasizes the role of government policies as catalysts for economic recovery. Readers will explore how strategic policy decisions, such as the GI Bill, played a pivotal role in shaping the post-war economic landscape. Real-life examples highlight the potential of well-designed government interventions to stimulate economic growth.

Section 5: Strategies for Success - Applying Historical Insights

Lifelong Learning and Skill Development

This section provides practical strategies for individuals to enhance financial success based on the lessons from the Post-World War II Recession. Lifelong learning and skill development take center stage, offering a roadmap for adapting to changing economic demands. Real-life examples of individuals who embraced continuous learning serve as inspiration for contemporary career planning.

Entrepreneurial Spirit: Navigating Economic Shifts

Building on the theme of success strategies, this subsection encourages readers to embrace an entrepreneurial spirit in navigating economic shifts. By examining how businesses innovated and adapted during the post-war period, readers gain insights into the mindset and strategies that lead to success in dynamic and uncertain times.

Section 6: Navigating Economic Shifts with Confidence

Collaborative Economic Planning: A Framework for Success

The concluding section synthesizes the chapter's insights into a framework for navigating economic shifts with confidence. Readers will discover how collaborative economic planning, informed by historical wisdom, adaptability, and strategic government interventions, can position individuals and nations for success. The chapter closes with a call to action, urging readers to apply the lessons from the Post-World War II Recession to build resilient and prosperous financial futures.

The Post-World War II Recession (1945-1946)

Section 1: Transitioning from Wartime to Peacetime

The War's Economic Legacy

The chapter opens by exploring the economic landscape at the conclusion of World War II, marked by the triumph of Allied forces and the significant transformations in wartime production. Readers will delve into the unique challenges of transitioning from a wartime economy, where production was geared towards military needs, to a peacetime economy with a focus on rebuilding and readjustment.

Demobilization and Economic Realities

This section examines the process of demobilization, as millions of soldiers returned home, war industries scaled back, and wartime contracts came to an end. The chapter sheds light on the economic realities of this transition, including the challenges of absorbing returning veterans into the workforce and shifting production from wartime necessities to consumer goods.

Section 2: The Short-Lived Recession

Economic Contraction and Government Intervention

This section delves into the short-lived recession that occurred in the immediate aftermath of World War II. Readers will explore the factors contributing to the economic contraction, including the temporary slowdown in government spending, as war-related expenditures decreased. The chapter analyzes the role of government intervention in stabilizing the economy during this brief downturn.

The GI Bill and Economic Revival

Building on the discussion of government intervention, this subsection highlights the positive impact of policies such as the GI Bill. Readers will gain insights into how the GI Bill, designed to support returning veterans with education, housing, and employment benefits, played a crucial role in economic revival. The chapter examines the lasting legacy of such policies in shaping post-war prosperity.

Section 3: Employment Shifts and Industrial Adaptation

Employment Challenges and Labor Dynamics

This section explores the employment shifts and labor dynamics during the post-war period. Readers will gain insights into the challenges of reintegrating veterans into the civilian workforce and the changing dynamics of industrial employment. Real-life stories and case studies illuminate the experiences of individuals and industries adapting to the peacetime economy.

Industrial Adaptation and Innovation

Building on the discussion of employment shifts, this subsection examines how industries adapted to the new economic realities. Readers will explore the innovations and adaptations that fueled post-war industrial growth, from technological advancements to shifts in production focus. The chapter analyzes the entrepreneurial spirit that emerged during this period and its relevance to contemporary economic transformations.

Section 4: Lessons for Today - Applying Historical Wisdom

Economic Resilience through Adaptability

This section synthesizes lessons from the Post-World War II Recession and applies them to contemporary financial landscapes. Readers will discover how economic resilience through adaptability became a cornerstone of post-war recovery. Insights from historical experiences provide a guide for individuals and businesses in navigating economic shifts and uncertainties.

Government Policies as Catalysts for Economic Recovery

Building on the theme of financial wisdom, this subsection emphasizes the role of government policies as catalysts for economic recovery. Readers will explore how strategic policy decisions, such as the GI Bill, played a pivotal role in shaping the post-war economic landscape. Real-life examples highlight the potential of well-designed government interventions to stimulate economic growth.

Section 5: Strategies for Success - Applying Historical Insights

Lifelong Learning and Skill Development

This section provides practical strategies for individuals to enhance financial success based on the lessons from the Post-World War II Recession. Lifelong learning and skill development take center stage, offering a roadmap for adapting to changing economic demands. Real-life examples of individuals who embraced continuous learning serve as inspiration for contemporary career planning.

Entrepreneurial Spirit: Navigating Economic Shifts

Building on the theme of success strategies, this subsection encourages readers to embrace an entrepreneurial spirit in navigating economic shifts. By examining how businesses innovated and adapted during the post-war period, readers gain insights into the mindset and strategies that lead to success in dynamic and uncertain times.

Section 6: Navigating Economic Shifts with Confidence

Collaborative Economic Planning: A Framework for Success

The concluding section synthesizes the chapter's insights into a framework for navigating economic shifts with confidence. Readers will discover how collaborative economic planning, informed by historical wisdom, adaptability, and strategic government interventions, can position individuals and nations for success. The chapter closes with a call to action, urging readers to apply the lessons from the Post-World War II Recession to build resilient and prosperous financial futures.

In Chapter 3, readers embark on a journey through the unique challenges and lessons of the Post-World War II Recession, gaining valuable insights into the factors that shaped this transitional economic period. By examining historical lessons, applying them to contemporary financial landscapes, and synthesizing success strategies, readers are equipped to navigate economic shifts with confidence, resilience, and a strategic mindset.

User

can you write Chapter 3 using the example of the COVID-19 Pandemic Recession (2020): The global economic downturn caused by the COVID-19 pandemic, marked by widespread lockdowns, supply chain disruptions, and a decline in consumer spending. and tell was what we can learn from it and how to manage your finances and be successful now using the given example

ChatGPT

Chapter 3: Learning from the Present - The COVID-19 Pandemic Recession (2020)

Section 1: Unprecedented Disruption and Economic Turmoil

The Global Shockwave

The chapter unfolds against the backdrop of the unprecedented COVID-19 pandemic, which sent shockwaves through global economies. Readers will delve into the sudden onset of lockdowns, supply chain disruptions, and a sharp decline in consumer spending that characterized the pandemic-induced recession. The chapter sets the stage by exploring the unique challenges posed by a health crisis-turned-economic downturn.

The Anatomy of Economic Disruption

This section dissects the multifaceted impacts of the COVID-19 pandemic on the economy, from business closures and layoffs to disruptions in international trade and financial markets. Real-world examples and case studies illuminate the ways in which the pandemic-induced recession differed from previous economic downturns, emphasizing its rapid and widespread nature.

Section 2: Remote Work, Digital Transformation, and Changing Consumer Behavior

The Acceleration of Digital Trends

This section explores how the pandemic accelerated pre-existing trends, such as remote work and digital transformation. Readers will gain insights into the rapid adoption of remote work technologies, e-commerce, and digital services as businesses and consumers adapted to the new normal. The chapter examines the transformative impact of these changes on industries and individuals alike.

Shifting Consumer Preferences and Spending Patterns

Building on the discussion of digital transformation, this subsection delves into how the pandemic reshaped consumer preferences and spending patterns. Readers will explore the rise of online shopping, the demand for home-based entertainment, and the implications for industries that successfully adapted to changing consumer behavior. The chapter analyzes the lessons for businesses and individuals in navigating evolving market dynamics.

Section 3: Government Responses and Economic Resilience

Unprecedented Fiscal Stimulus

This section explores the unprecedented fiscal stimulus measures implemented by governments worldwide to counter the economic impact of the pandemic. Readers will gain insights into stimulus packages, unemployment benefits, and business support programs designed to mitigate the financial fallout. The chapter analyzes the effectiveness of these interventions and their implications for economic resilience.

The Role of Global Cooperation

Building on the discussion of government responses, this subsection emphasizes the importance of global cooperation in addressing the pandemic-induced recession. Readers will explore collaborative efforts among nations, international organizations, and the private sector to combat the economic fallout. The chapter examines the significance of coordinated responses in fostering global economic stability.

Section 4: Lessons for Today - Adapting to Uncertainty

Financial Preparedness and Emergency Funds

This section synthesizes lessons from the COVID-19 Pandemic Recession and applies them to contemporary financial landscapes.

Readers will discover the importance of financial preparedness and building emergency funds as a buffer against unforeseen economic shocks. Insights from individuals who navigated the crisis with financial resilience provide a guide for managing personal finances in uncertain times.

Embracing Technological Adaptation

Building on the theme of financial wisdom, this subsection highlights the value of embracing technological adaptation. Readers will explore how individuals and businesses that quickly adapted to digital trends during the pandemic were better positioned for success. Real-life examples showcase the transformative power of technology in enhancing economic resilience.

Section 5: Strategies for Success - Navigating Uncertainty

Continuous Learning and Skill Development

This section provides practical strategies for individuals to enhance financial success based on the lessons from the pandemic-induced recession. Continuous learning and skill development take center stage, offering a roadmap for staying relevant in a rapidly evolving economic landscape. Real-life examples of individuals who embraced continuous learning serve as inspiration for contemporary career planning.

Entrepreneurial Innovation and Agility

Building on the theme of success strategies, this subsection encourages readers to embrace entrepreneurial innovation and agility. By examining how businesses innovated and adapted during the pandemic, readers gain insights into the mindset and strategies that lead to success in dynamic and uncertain times.

Section 6: Navigating Economic Shifts with Confidence

Collective Resilience and Social Responsibility: A Framework for Success

The concluding section synthesizes the chapter's insights into a framework for navigating economic shifts with confidence. Readers will discover how collective resilience, social responsibility, and individual adaptability can collectively position society for success. The chapter closes with a call to action, urging readers to apply the lessons from the COVID-19 Pandemic Recession to build resilient and prosperous financial futures.

Chapter 4: Digital Assets in Downturns

Section 1: The Rise of Digital Assets

In the dynamic landscape of contemporary investments, traditional paradigms are undergoing a radical transformation with the ascent of digital assets. This chapter delves into the emergence of cryptocurrencies, non-fungible tokens (NFTs), and other digital assets, shedding light on their role as a compelling frontier for investors navigating economic downturns.

Shifting Investment Paradigms

The conventional approaches to investing are expanding to encompass the realm of digital assets, presenting investors with a tantalizing avenue for diversification. This section explores how digital assets, characterized by their limited correlation with traditional markets, offer a unique strategy for risk management and potential returns.

Diversification in the Digital Era

Navigating the landscape of digital assets is integral for investors seeking to fortify their portfolios. The chapter delves into how these assets, ranging from cryptocurrencies to NFTs, contribute to a diversified and resilient investment strategy in the face of economic challenges.

Section 2: Navigating Economic Challenges with Digital Art

Digital Art as an Alternative Investment

Amid economic downturns, investors are increasingly exploring unconventional assets, and digital art takes center stage as a unique alternative investment. This section scrutinizes the role of digital art, particularly in the form of NFTs, as an unconventional yet promising investment avenue. The chapter explores the intersection of technology, art, and finance, shaping a novel investment landscape.

Case Studies of Digital Art Success

Real-world examples spotlight successful digital art investments, offering insights into the potential for value appreciation within this space. Through case studies, readers gain an understanding of the factors contributing to the success of digital art as an investment during economic challenges.

Section 3: Blockchain Technology and Decentralized Finance (DeFi)

The Promise of Blockchain

This section delves into the revolutionary potential of blockchain, the foundational technology for many digital assets. Readers will gain insights into how blockchain provides transparency, security, and decentralization, fundamentally reshaping traditional financial systems.

Decentralized Finance Strategies

Building on the discussion of blockchain, the chapter unfolds the concept of decentralized finance (DeFi). Readers will explore strategies within DeFi, such as decentralized exchanges, yield farming, and liquidity provision, presenting alternative approaches to traditional financial instruments.

Section 4: Risk Considerations and Regulatory Landscape

Managing Risks in the Digital Frontier

As digital assets present new opportunities, comprehending and managing associated risks becomes paramount. This section delves into considerations such as market volatility, security risks, and regulatory uncertainties. The chapter provides insights into risk mitigation strategies and responsible investing practices in the evolving digital landscape.

Regulatory Developments in Digital Finance

In the ever-evolving digital asset space, the regulatory landscape is equally dynamic. Readers will gain insights into how governments and regulatory bodies respond to the growing prominence of digital assets. The chapter analyzes the implications of regulatory changes for investors and the broader financial ecosystem.

Section 5: Strategies for Success - Balancing Tradition and Innovation

Integrating Digital Assets into Portfolios

Practical strategies for seamlessly integrating digital assets into investment portfolios are outlined in this section. Readers will discover how to strike a balance between traditional and digital assets, considering risk tolerance, investment goals, and market dynamics. Real-life examples highlight successful portfolios that blend both worlds strategically.

The Mindset of Digital Investors

Success in the digital asset space requires a specific mindset. This subsection explores the adaptability, research diligence, and long-term perspective required for success. Through the stories of individuals who navigated economic downturns with a forward-thinking approach to digital investments, readers gain insights into the mindset of successful digital investors.

Section 6: Charting the Future of Digital Finance

Evolving Investment Landscapes: A Framework for Success

The concluding section synthesizes the chapter's insights into a framework for navigating economic downturns with digital assets. Readers will discover how understanding the evolving investment landscapes, embracing digital innovation, and adopting a diversified approach can position individuals for success. The chapter closes with a call to action, urging readers to explore the dynamic opportunities presented by digital assets in the ever-changing financial frontier.

Section 7: Cryptocurrencies and Market Dynamics

The Role of Cryptocurrencies

This section further explores the role of cryptocurrencies in navigating economic challenges. Readers will gain insights into how cryptocurrencies, with Bitcoin as a prominent example, have emerged as both a store of value and a speculative asset. The chapter delves into the unique market behavior and volatility of the crypto space.

Market Behavior and Crypto Volatility

Building on the discussion of cryptocurrencies, this subsection delves into the distinctive market behavior and volatility within the crypto space. Readers will explore the factors influencing price movements, the impact of market sentiment, and strategies for managing risks in a volatile environment. Real-life examples showcase instances where investors successfully navigated the dynamic crypto market.

Section 8: Tokenization and Real-world Assets

Tokenization as a Financial Innovation

This section introduces the concept of tokenization, wherein real-world assets are represented digitally on blockchain platforms. Readers will explore how tokenization can democratize access to traditionally illiquid assets, such as real estate and artworks. The chapter analyzes the potential benefits of tokenization for investors seeking to diversify their portfolios with fractional ownership of tangible assets.

Case Studies of Tokenized Assets

Building on the discussion of tokenization, this subsection presents case studies of successful tokenized asset projects. Readers will explore instances where real estate, art, and other tangible assets were successfully tokenized, providing liquidity and access to a broader investor base. The chapter highlights the transformative potential of tokenization in reshaping traditional investment structures.

Section 9: NFTs and the Digital Ownership Revolution

The Rise of Non-Fungible Tokens (NFTs)

This section explores the phenomenon of Non-Fungible Tokens (NFTs), unique digital assets that represent ownership or proof of authenticity for digital or physical items. Readers will gain insights into how NFTs have revolutionized digital ownership, with applications in art, gaming, and entertainment. The chapter examines the market dynamics and considerations for investors interested in NFTs.

Success Stories in the NFT Space

Building on the discussion of NFTs, this subsection presents success stories of individuals and artists who thrived in the NFT space. Readers will explore instances where digital creators monetized their work through NFT sales, reshaping the traditional model of content ownership. The chapter showcases the diverse opportunities and challenges within the NFT ecosystem.

Section 10: Ethical Considerations and Sustainable Investing

Ethical Dimensions of Digital Finance

This section delves into the ethical considerations associated with digital assets and blockchain technologies. Readers will explore topics such as environmental sustainability, ethical sourcing of digital assets, and the social impact of decentralized finance. The chapter emphasizes the importance of ethical considerations in shaping responsible and sustainable investment practices.

The Role of Sustainable Investing

Building on the discussion of ethics, this subsection examines the role of sustainable investing in the digital finance space. Readers will gain insights into how investors can align their values with their investment choices, considering environmental, social, and governance (ESG) criteria. Real-life examples showcase projects and initiatives that promote sustainability within the digital asset ecosystem.

Section 11: Strategies for Success - Blending Tradition and Innovation

Dynamic Portfolio Management

This section provides practical strategies for individuals seeking to blend traditional and digital assets in their portfolios. Readers will discover how dynamic portfolio management, informed by market research, risk analysis, and a forward-looking approach, can optimize returns and mitigate risks. Real-life examples highlight successful investors who strategically combined traditional and digital assets.

Educating for Financial Literacy in the Digital Age

Building on the theme of success strategies, this subsection emphasizes the importance of financial literacy in the digital age. Readers will explore the knowledge and skills required to navigate the complexities of digital assets, blockchain, and decentralized finance. The chapter showcases initiatives and educational resources that empower individuals to make informed and confident investment decisions.

Section 12: Shaping the Future of Digital Finance

Technological Evolution and Financial Inclusion: A Framework for Success

The concluding section synthesizes the chapter's insights into a framework for navigating economic downturns with digital assets. Readers will discover how technological evolution, ethical considerations, and a strategic blend of traditional and digital assets can position individuals for success. The chapter closes with a call to action, urging readers to explore the dynamic opportunities presented by digital assets in the ever-changing financial frontier.

Section 13: The Future Landscape of Digital Assets

Innovations on the Horizon

This section explores emerging innovations in the digital asset space, providing readers with a glimpse into the future. Topics such as decentralized identity, tokenized securities, and advancements in blockchain technology are discussed. The chapter highlights how ongoing developments contribute to the maturation and expansion of the digital finance ecosystem.

The Role of Artificial Intelligence in Digital Finance

Building on the discussion of innovations, this subsection examines the role of artificial intelligence (AI) in shaping the future of digital finance. Readers will gain insights into how AI-driven algorithms and machine learning models can enhance investment strategies, risk management, and overall decision-making in the digital asset landscape. Real-life examples showcase the transformative potential of AI in financial services.

Section 14: Practical Implementation and Security Measures

Secure Practices in Digital Asset Management

This section provides practical guidance on securely managing digital assets. Readers will explore topics such as private key management, secure wallets, and best practices for safeguarding digital investments. The chapter emphasizes the importance of security measures to protect against cyber threats and ensure the integrity of digital assets.

Regulatory Compliance in Digital Finance

Building on the discussion of security, this subsection delves into the regulatory landscape of digital finance. Readers will gain insights into the evolving regulatory frameworks governing digital assets, including compliance requirements and considerations for investors. The chapter examines the importance of adhering to regulatory standards to ensure a secure and legally compliant digital asset environment.

Section 15: The Intersection of Traditional Finance and Digital Assets

Collaboration and Integration

This section explores the potential for collaboration and integration between traditional finance and digital assets. Readers will gain insights into how traditional financial institutions are incorporating digital assets into their offerings, from cryptocurrency trading desks to blockchain-based financial products. The chapter highlights the synergies and challenges associated with the convergence of traditional and digital finance.

Hybrid Approaches to Investment

Building on the discussion of collaboration, this subsection examines hybrid approaches to investment that seamlessly blend traditional and digital assets. Readers will explore how diversified portfolios can leverage the strengths of both worlds, capitalizing on the stability of traditional investments and the growth potential of digital assets. Real-life examples showcase successful hybrid investment strategies.

Section 16: Navigating the Dynamic Landscape

Continuous Learning and Adaptability: A Framework for Success

The concluding section synthesizes the chapter's insights into a framework for navigating the dynamic landscape of digital assets. Readers will discover how continuous learning, adaptability, and a strategic blend of traditional and digital assets can position individuals for success. The chapter closes with a call to action, urging readers to stay informed, embrace innovation, and actively participate in the ongoing evolution of the financial landscape.

Section 17: Building Resilience in the Digital Era

The Importance of Resilience

This section emphasizes the critical role of resilience in navigating the ever-changing digital landscape. Readers will explore how building resilience, both at the individual and institutional levels, becomes a cornerstone for success in the dynamic world of digital assets. Real-world examples illustrate how resilience can help weather uncertainties and downturns.

Adapting to Technological Shifts

Building on the theme of resilience, this subsection explores the necessity of adapting to technological shifts. Readers will gain insights into the rapid pace of technological advancements within the digital asset space and how staying informed and agile is key to capitalizing on emerging opportunities. The chapter examines strategies for continuous adaptation in the face of technological evolution.

Section 18: Democratizing Finance through Decentralization

The Vision of Decentralization

This section delves into the concept of decentralization as a driving force behind digital assets. Readers will explore how decentralized finance (DeFi) and blockchain technologies aim to democratize access to financial services, reduce reliance on traditional intermediaries, and empower individuals globally. The chapter examines the transformative potential of decentralization in reshaping financial systems.

Inclusive Financial Systems

Building on the discussion of decentralization, this subsection highlights the potential for inclusive financial systems enabled by digital assets. Readers will gain insights into how decentralized finance projects and blockchain technologies can address issues of financial exclusion, providing access to banking services, investments, and economic opportunities for underserved populations.

Section 19: Ethical Investing in the Digital Age

Ethical Considerations in Digital Finance

This section explores the ethical considerations associated with digital assets and blockchain technologies. Readers will examine topics such as privacy, security, and the social impact of decentralized finance. The chapter emphasizes the importance of ethical investing in the digital age, urging investors to consider the broader societal implications of their financial choices.

Impact Investing and Social Responsibility

Building on the discussion of ethics, this subsection delves into the concept of impact investing and social responsibility within the digital asset space. Readers will explore how investments in projects with positive social and environmental outcomes contribute to a more sustainable and responsible financial ecosystem. Real-life examples showcase impactful initiatives in the realm of digital finance.

Section 20: Future Challenges and Opportunities

Anticipating Challenges

This section addresses potential challenges that may arise in the future of digital assets. Readers will explore considerations such as regulatory developments, technological risks, and market uncertainties. The chapter examines strategies for anticipating challenges and positioning oneself to navigate the evolving landscape successfully.

Seizing Opportunities

Building on the discussion of challenges, this subsection emphasizes the importance of seizing opportunities within the digital asset space. Readers will gain insights into identifying emerging trends, innovative projects, and market niches that present growth potential. Real-life examples showcase individuals and businesses that proactively seized opportunities amid uncertainties.

Section 21: Shaping a Vision for Digital Finance

The Collaborative Evolution: A Framework for Success

The concluding section synthesizes the chapter's insights into a framework for navigating economic downturns with digital assets. Readers will discover how collaborative evolution, ethical considerations, and a commitment to resilience can collectively position individuals and societies for success. The chapter closes with a call to action, urging readers to actively contribute to shaping a vision for a sustainable and inclusive future in the digital finance era.

Chapter 5: Market Behavior During Recessions

Section 1: Introduction to Market Dynamics

Understanding Economic Cycles

This section sets the stage by introducing readers to the concept of economic cycles and their impact on financial markets. Exploring the dynamics of expansions and contractions, readers will gain a foundational understanding of how market behavior is intricately tied to the broader economic landscape.

The Role of Sentiment in Markets

Building on the discussion of economic cycles, this subsection delves into the psychological aspects of market behavior. Readers will explore how investor sentiment, shaped by factors such as fear, greed, and uncertainty, plays a pivotal role in driving market movements. Real-world examples illustrate the profound impact of sentiment on financial markets.

Section 2: Historical Perspectives on Market Movements

Lessons from Previous Recessions

This section examines historical recessions, drawing insights from past market movements during economic downturns. By analyzing events such as the Great Depression, the Dot-Com Bubble Burst, and the Global Financial Crisis, readers will gain a nuanced understanding of how markets have historically responded to challenging economic conditions.

Market Volatility and Risk

Building on the exploration of historical recessions, this subsection delves into the concepts of market volatility and risk. Readers will explore how heightened volatility often accompanies economic downturns, presenting both challenges and opportunities for investors. The chapter provides strategies for navigating turbulent markets and managing risks effectively.

Section 3: Factors Influencing Market Behavior During Recessions

Macroeconomic Indicators

This section explores key macroeconomic indicators that significantly influence market behavior during recessions. Readers will gain insights into metrics such as GDP growth, unemployment rates, and inflation, understanding how these factors contribute to the overall economic landscape and shape investor sentiment.

Central Bank Policies

Building on the discussion of macroeconomic indicators, this subsection examines the role of central bank policies in influencing market dynamics. Readers will explore how interest rate decisions, monetary policy, and interventions by central banks impact investor confidence, borrowing costs, and overall market stability.

Section 4: Behavioral Finance and Market Anomalies

The Psychology of Investing

This section introduces the field of behavioral finance, exploring how cognitive biases and psychological factors impact investment decisions. Readers will gain insights into phenomena such as herding behavior, overreaction, and underreaction, understanding how these behavioral traits contribute to market anomalies during recessions.

Exploiting Market Anomalies

Building on the discussion of behavioral finance, this subsection examines the concept of exploiting market anomalies for strategic investment opportunities. The chapter provides examples of successful investment strategies that leverage behavioral biases and market inefficiencies, offering readers practical insights into navigating markets during economic downturns.

Section 5: Asset Classes and Sectoral Responses

Equities and Fixed Income

This section explores how different asset classes respond to economic recessions. Readers will gain insights into the behavior of equities and fixed income instruments, understanding how these traditional investments react to changing economic conditions and market sentiment.

Sectoral Winners and Losers

Building on the discussion of asset classes, this subsection delves into sectoral responses during recessions. Readers will explore which industries tend to thrive and which face challenges during economic downturns. Real-life case studies showcase sectoral winners and losers, providing valuable insights for strategic investment decisions.

Section 6: The Role of Technology in Shaping Market Behavior

Technological Innovations in Financial Markets

This section explores how technology has transformed financial markets, influencing market behavior and investment strategies. Readers will gain insights into innovations such as algorithmic trading, high-frequency trading, and the impact of technology on market liquidity and efficiency.

Digital Transformation in Finance

Building on the discussion of technological innovations, this subsection examines the broader digital transformation in finance. Readers will explore the role of fintech, blockchain, and artificial intelligence in shaping market dynamics during economic downturns. Real-world examples showcase the disruptive potential of technological advancements in financial markets.

Section 7: Investment Strategies in Volatile Markets

Tactical Asset Allocation

This section introduces tactical asset allocation as a strategy for navigating volatile markets. Readers will explore how adjusting portfolio allocations based on short-term market conditions can enhance returns and manage risks during economic recessions. Practical implementation and case studies illustrate the effectiveness of this strategy.

Risk Hedging Strategies

Building on the discussion of tactical asset allocation, this subsection delves into specific risk hedging strategies. Readers will gain insights into techniques such as options trading, futures contracts, and other derivatives that can be employed to protect portfolios from downside risks in turbulent markets.

Section 8: Behavioral Resilience in Market Fluctuations

Emotional Intelligence in Investing

This section emphasizes the importance of emotional intelligence in maintaining resilience during market fluctuations. Readers will explore strategies for managing emotions such as fear and greed, understanding how a disciplined and emotionally resilient approach can contribute to long-term investment success.

Learning from Market Mistakes

Building on the discussion of emotional intelligence, this subsection explores the concept of learning from market mistakes. Readers will gain insights from real-life examples of investors who navigated through market downturns, learning valuable lessons that contributed to their overall success.

Section 9: Case Studies: Notable Market Movements

The 2008 Financial Crisis

This section provides an in-depth analysis of the 2008 financial crisis, examining the market movements, key factors, and lessons learned from one of the most significant economic downturns in recent history.

The COVID-19 Pandemic

Building on the exploration of historical market movements, this subsection analyzes the market dynamics during the COVID-19 pandemic. Readers will gain insights into how the pandemic-induced economic downturn influenced global markets and investor behavior.

Section 10: Looking Ahead - Adapting to Future Market Challenges

The Future of Financial Markets

This section explores the potential evolution of financial markets in the coming years. Readers will delve into discussions on emerging trends, technological advancements, and potential challenges that may shape future market behavior during economic downturns.

Sustainable Investing and ESG Factors

Building on the discussion of the future, this subsection explores the growing significance of sustainable investing and Environmental, Social, and Governance (ESG) factors. Readers will gain insights into how considerations of environmental impact, social responsibility, and corporate governance are influencing investment decisions and market behavior.

Fintech Innovations and Disruptions

This section delves into the continued influence of fintech innovations on financial markets. Readers will explore how advancements in financial technology, including blockchain, decentralized finance (DeFi), and digital currencies, may reshape market dynamics and investment strategies in the coming years.

Section 11: Expert Perspectives on Market Behavior

Insights from Seasoned Investors

This section gathers perspectives from seasoned investors, economists, and financial experts. Readers will benefit from firsthand accounts, lessons learned, and strategies employed by experts who have navigated various economic downturns. Real-life anecdotes and interviews provide a unique glimpse into the mindset of successful investors during turbulent market conditions.

The Role of Research and Analysis

Building on expert perspectives, this subsection emphasizes the importance of research and analysis in understanding market behavior. Readers will gain insights into how rigorous research, data analysis, and informed decision-making contribute to successful investment strategies during recessions.

Section 12: Conclusion - Navigating the Rollercoaster

Synthesizing Key Insights

This concluding section synthesizes key insights from the chapter, offering a comprehensive overview of market behavior during economic downturns. Readers will recap foundational concepts, strategies, and expert perspectives discussed throughout the chapter.

Encouraging Resilience and Adaptability

The chapter concludes with a call to action, encouraging readers to cultivate resilience and adaptability in their approach to investing. Recognizing that market behavior is inherently dynamic, the chapter emphasizes the importance of continuous learning, staying informed, and adapting strategies to navigate the inevitable fluctuations in financial markets.

A Framework for Thriving in Turbulent Times

The conclusion provides a framework for thriving in turbulent times, combining emotional resilience, strategic investment approaches, and a forward-looking mindset. By embracing these principles, readers are empowered to not only navigate the rollercoaster of market behavior during recessions but also position themselves for long-term success in the ever-evolving financial landscape.

Chapter 6: Emotional Resilience in Investing: Navigating the Rollercoaster

Section 1: Introduction to Emotional Resilience

The Psychological Challenges of Investing

This section sets the stage by addressing the psychological challenges investors face during market fluctuations. Readers will explore the emotional rollercoaster that often accompanies economic downturns and learn why developing emotional resilience is crucial for making informed and rational investment decisions.

Understanding Emotional Resilience

Building on the discussion of psychological challenges, this subsection introduces the concept of emotional resilience. Readers will gain insights into what emotional resilience entails, why it is essential for successful investing, and how individuals can cultivate this trait to navigate the ups and downs of financial markets.

Section 2: Embracing Uncertainty and Ambiguity

The Nature of Financial Uncertainty

This section delves into the inherent uncertainty of financial markets, especially during economic downturns. Readers will explore the factors contributing to uncertainty, such as unpredictable events, market sentiment, and global economic dynamics. The chapter provides strategies for embracing uncertainty and reframing it as an opportunity for informed decision-making.

The Power of Ambiguity

Building on the discussion of uncertainty, this subsection explores the related concept of ambiguity. Readers will learn how to navigate situations where information is incomplete or unclear, developing the ability to make reasoned decisions in ambiguous market conditions. Real-life examples illustrate instances where embracing ambiguity led to successful investment outcomes.

Section 3: Cognitive Biases and Decision-Making

The Impact of Cognitive Biases

This section introduces readers to cognitive biases and their influence on decision-making. By understanding common biases such as confirmation bias, loss aversion, and overconfidence, readers can identify and mitigate these biases to make more rational and objective investment decisions.

Strategies for Overcoming Biases

Building on the discussion of cognitive biases, this subsection provides practical strategies for overcoming biases in investment decision-making. Readers will explore techniques such as mindfulness, cognitive restructuring, and diverse perspectives to counteract the impact of biases on their financial choices.

Section 4: Developing a Mindful Approach to Investing

The Role of Mindfulness

This section explores the concept of mindfulness and its application to investing. Readers will gain insights into how practicing mindfulness can enhance self-awareness, emotional regulation, and decision-making, contributing to a more balanced and resilient approach to navigating market volatility.

Mindful Investment Practices

Building on the discussion of mindfulness, this subsection provides specific investment practices that incorporate mindfulness principles. Readers will learn how to apply mindfulness to activities such as portfolio review, risk assessment, and market analysis, fostering a more intentional and focused investment approach.

Section 5: Overcoming Fear and Greed in Market Fluctuations

The Impact of Fear and Greed

This section addresses two powerful emotions—fear and greed—that often drive market behavior. Readers will explore the psychological underpinnings of these emotions and understand how they can lead to impulsive decisions. The chapter provides insights into recognizing and mitigating the influence of fear and greed in investment choices.

Strategies for Emotional Regulation

Building on the discussion of fear and greed, this subsection offers practical strategies for emotional regulation. Readers will learn techniques for managing anxiety during market downturns and avoiding overexuberance in times of market euphoria. Real-life examples illustrate how emotional regulation contributes to sound investment practices.

Section 6: Building Resilience Through Learning

The Growth Mindset in Investing

This section introduces the concept of the growth mindset and its relevance to investing. Readers will explore how adopting a growth mindset—viewing challenges as opportunities to learn and grow—can contribute to resilience in the face of market uncertainties.

Continuous Learning and Adaptation

Building on the discussion of the growth mindset, this subsection emphasizes the importance of continuous learning in building emotional resilience. Readers will gain insights into how staying informed, seeking diverse perspectives, and adapting to new market realities contribute to long-term success in investing.

Section 7: Expert Insights on Emotional Resilience

Perspectives from Seasoned Investors

This section gathers perspectives from seasoned investors who have navigated through various market cycles. Readers will benefit from the wisdom and experiences of these experts, gaining insights into how emotional resilience played a pivotal role in their investment journeys.

Strategies Employed During Market Challenges

Building on expert insights, this subsection explores specific strategies employed by seasoned investors to maintain emotional resilience during market challenges. Real-life anecdotes and case studies provide practical examples of how investors successfully weathered financial storms by staying emotionally resilient.

Section 8: Cultivating Patience in a Fast-paced World

The Impatience Challenge

This section explores the challenge of impatience in the fast-paced world of investing. Readers will understand how the desire for quick returns and instant gratification can lead to impulsive decision-making. The chapter provides strategies for cultivating patience, emphasizing the importance of a long-term perspective.

The Virtue of Patience

Building on the discussion of impatience, this subsection highlights the virtue of patience in investing. Readers will explore how patient investors are better positioned to weather market downturns, capitalize on opportunities, and achieve sustainable long-term growth. Real-life examples illustrate the rewards of patient investing.

Section 9: Building a Diversified and Resilient Portfolio

The Role of Diversification

This section emphasizes the role of diversification in building a resilient portfolio. Readers will gain insights into how diversifying across asset classes, industries, and geographic regions can mitigate risks and enhance overall portfolio resilience during economic uncertainties.

Tailoring Portfolios to Risk Tolerance

Building on the discussion of diversification, this subsection explores the importance of tailoring portfolios to individual risk tolerance. Readers will learn how aligning investments with risk preferences contributes to emotional resilience, allowing investors to navigate market fluctuations with greater confidence.

Section 10: Staying Informed Without Overwhelm

Information Overload Challenges

This section addresses the challenges of information overload in the digital age. Readers will explore how the constant stream of financial news, market analyses, and investment advice can contribute to anxiety and decision paralysis. The chapter provides strategies for staying informed without succumbing to overwhelm.

Curating Information Sources

Building on the discussion of information overload, this subsection offers practical tips for curating information sources. Readers will learn how to filter through the noise, focus on reputable and relevant sources, and maintain a balanced perspective. Real-life examples illustrate how a curated approach to information enhances decision-making.

Section 11: Navigating Market Sentiment and Social Media Influence

The Impact of Market Sentiment

This section delves into the influence of market sentiment on investor behavior. Readers will gain insights into how social media, online forums, and collective investor sentiment can drive market movements. The chapter provides strategies for navigating and interpreting market sentiment without being swayed by irrational exuberance or panic.

Balancing Social Media Engagement

Building on the discussion of market sentiment, this subsection explores the role of social media in shaping investor perceptions. Readers will learn how to balance social media engagement, leverage valuable insights, and avoid succumbing to the herd mentality. Case studies illustrate instances where social media influence impacted market behavior.

Section 12: Resilience in the Face of Unexpected Events

Responding to Black Swan Events

This section addresses the concept of black swan events—unpredictable and extreme occurrences with significant consequences. Readers will explore strategies for building resilience to unexpected events, adapting investment approaches, and incorporating scenario planning into their overall strategy.

Thriving Amidst Economic and Global Challenges

Building on the discussion of black swan events, this subsection examines how investors can thrive amidst economic and global challenges. Real-life examples showcase individuals and institutions that demonstrated resilience during times of crisis, highlighting the importance of adaptability and forward-thinking.

Section 13: The Role of Mentorship in Building Resilience

Seeking Guidance from Mentors

This section highlights the value of mentorship in cultivating emotional resilience. Readers will explore how seeking guidance from experienced mentors can provide insights, perspective, and emotional support during challenging market conditions. The chapter provides tips for finding suitable mentors and establishing meaningful mentor-mentee relationships.

Mentoring Others: A Two-way Street

Building on the discussion of mentorship, this subsection emphasizes the reciprocal nature of mentoring. Readers will learn how mentoring others can enhance one's own emotional resilience, contribute to a sense of purpose, and foster a supportive community of investors.

Section 14: Harnessing Emotional Intelligence for Investment Success

Understanding Emotional Intelligence

This section explores the concept of emotional intelligence and its direct impact on investment success. Readers will gain insights into the five components of emotional intelligence—self-awareness, self-regulation, motivation, empathy, and social skills—and how developing these attributes contributes to making sound investment decisions.

Practical Applications of Emotional Intelligence

Building on the discussion of emotional intelligence, this subsection provides practical applications for incorporating emotional intelligence into investment practices. Readers will learn how to apply emotional intelligence in areas such as risk management, decision-making, and building constructive relationships with financial advisors and fellow investors.

Section 15: The Psychological Resilience Toolkit

Building a Resilience Toolkit

This section introduces readers to a psychological resilience toolkit tailored for investors. The toolkit encompasses various strategies, exercises, and practices aimed at enhancing emotional resilience. From mindfulness exercises to visualization techniques, readers will discover a range of tools they can integrate into their daily routines.

Journaling for Reflection and Growth

Building on the resilience toolkit, this subsection explores the benefits of journaling for reflection and growth. Readers will learn how keeping an investment journal can serve as a valuable tool for tracking emotions, analyzing decisions, and fostering a continuous learning mindset. Real-life examples demonstrate the transformative power of reflective journaling.

Section 16: Balancing Conviction with Adaptability

The Challenge of Balancing Conviction

This section addresses the delicate balance between maintaining conviction in one's investment thesis and being adaptable to changing market conditions. Readers will explore how rigid adherence to a plan can sometimes clash with the need for flexibility. The chapter provides strategies for finding the equilibrium between conviction and adaptability.

Flexibility in Investment Strategies

Building on the discussion of balance, this subsection delves into the importance of flexibility in investment strategies. Readers will gain insights into how adapting strategies based on evolving market conditions can be a strength rather than a weakness. Real-life examples illustrate instances where flexibility contributed to investment success.

Section 17: Nurturing a Positive Investor Mindset

The Power of Positivity

This section explores the impact of a positive mindset on investment success. Readers will gain insights into how maintaining a positive and optimistic outlook can influence decision-making, resilience, and the ability to seize opportunities even in challenging market conditions.

Strategies for Cultivating Positivity

Building on the discussion of positivity, this subsection provides practical strategies for cultivating and nurturing a positive investor mindset. From gratitude practices to constructive self-talk, readers will discover actionable techniques for fostering a resilient and optimistic approach to investing.

Section 18: Resilience in the Face of Loss

Coping with Investment Losses

This section addresses the emotional challenges associated with investment losses. Readers will explore strategies for coping with losses, reframing setbacks as learning opportunities, and avoiding the psychological pitfalls that can accompany financial downturns.

The Psychological Recovery Process

Building on the discussion of coping with losses, this subsection delves into the psychological recovery process after experiencing setbacks in investing. Readers will gain insights into the stages of recovery, from acknowledging emotions to rebuilding confidence and adapting strategies for future success.

Section 19: Expert Perspectives on Emotional Resilience

Interviews with Seasoned Investors

This section presents interviews with seasoned investors who share their perspectives on emotional resilience. Readers will benefit from the firsthand accounts of these experts, gaining insights into the challenges they faced, the strategies they employed, and the role of emotional resilience in their investment journeys.

Key Lessons Learned

Building on expert perspectives, this subsection distills key lessons learned from seasoned investors regarding emotional resilience. Readers will gain valuable takeaways, actionable advice, and a deeper understanding of the mindset required to navigate the emotional rollercoaster of investing successfully.

Section 20: conclusion of chapter 6

Synthesizing Key Insights:

The conclusion opens with the crucial task of synthesizing key insights from the chapter. It acts as a recapitulation, ensuring that readers have a clear understanding of the foundational concepts, strategies, and expert perspectives discussed throughout the entire chapter. This initial step aims to provide readers with a holistic view of the importance of emotional resilience in the context of investing during economic downturns.

Encouraging a Resilient Investor Mindset:

Following the synthesis, the chapter takes a proactive approach by issuing a call to action. It encourages readers to cultivate a resilient investor mindset. This mindset, it suggests, can be nurtured through the embrace of emotional resilience, continuous learning, and a growth-oriented perspective. By instilling these qualities, individuals are better equipped to confront and overcome the inevitable challenges and uncertainties inherent in financial markets.

A Framework for Thriving in Uncertain Times:

The core of the conclusion introduces a framework designed to guide readers through the tumultuous landscape of uncertain times. This framework combines emotional resilience, mindfulness, and a commitment to continuous learning. By adopting this multifaceted approach, readers are not only prepared to navigate the emotional rollercoaster of investing during economic downturns but also positioned to thrive and grow as resilient investors.

The Holistic Approach to Emotional Resilience:

The holistic nature of emotional resilience is underscored as the conclusion emphasizes that it extends beyond individual traits. It advocates for a balanced and comprehensive approach that encompasses diverse strategies and perspectives. This holistic perspective serves as a reminder that emotional resilience is not a one-size-fits-all concept, but rather a dynamic and adaptable quality that involves a combination of various elements.

Encouraging a Supportive Investment Community:

Recognizing the strength in unity, the chapter encourages readers to actively participate in a supportive investment community. By sharing experiences, insights, and support, investors contribute to the collective resilience of the community. This interconnectedness creates a robust ecosystem that can thrive despite the uncertainties posed by economic downturns.

The Ongoing Journey of Emotional Resilience:

To underscore the dynamic nature of emotional resilience, the concluding section reinforces the idea that it is an ongoing journey rather than a destination. Readers are encouraged to view emotional resilience as a skill that can be continually developed, refined, and applied throughout their entire investment journey. This perspective fosters a mindset of adaptability and continuous improvement.

A Holistic Framework for Investing Success:

In the final remarks, the chapter wraps up by presenting a holistic framework for investing success. This framework integrates emotional resilience, cognitive strategies, and a positive mindset. Readers are encouraged to embrace this comprehensive approach to navigate the unpredictable nature of financial markets and thrive in their investment endeavors.

Chapter 7: Investment Strategies During Recessions

Section 1: Introduction to Proactive Investing

The Proactive Mindset

This section establishes the importance of adopting a proactive mindset when navigating recessions. Readers will explore the mindset shift required to seize opportunities, adapt strategies, and position themselves for success amidst economic challenges.

The Pitfalls of Reactive Investing

Building on the discussion of proactive investing, this subsection highlights the pitfalls of reactive approaches. Readers will gain insights into common mistakes made by investors who react impulsively to market fluctuations, emphasizing the need for a strategic and proactive investment approach.

Section 2: Strategic Asset Allocation

The Foundation of Investment Strategy

This section introduces strategic asset allocation as the foundation of a recession-resilient investment strategy. Readers will explore the principles of diversification, risk management, and the strategic allocation of assets across different classes to optimize returns while mitigating risks.

Tailoring Portfolios to Economic Conditions

Building on the discussion of strategic asset allocation, this subsection delves into the importance of tailoring portfolios to specific economic conditions. Readers will gain insights into how adjusting asset allocations based on economic indicators can enhance portfolio resilience and performance during recessions.

Section 3: Defensive Investing Strategies

The Role of Defensive Investments

This section explores defensive investing strategies designed to protect portfolios during economic downturns. Readers will gain insights into defensive asset classes, such as bonds and dividend-paying stocks, and how these can serve as a shield against market volatility.

Hedging Against Market Risks

Building on the discussion of defensive investments, this subsection introduces hedging strategies to mitigate market risks. Readers will explore techniques such as options and futures contracts, designed to provide downside protection and enhance overall portfolio stability.

Section 4: Income-Generating Investments

The Importance of Income Generation

This section emphasizes the role of income-generating investments in recession-resilient portfolios. Readers will explore strategies for incorporating dividend stocks, bonds, and other income-producing assets to create a steady income stream during economic downturns.

Real Estate and Other Alternative Income Sources

Building on the discussion of income generation, this subsection explores alternative sources of income, such as real estate investments and peer-to-peer lending platforms. Readers will gain insights into diversifying income streams to enhance financial stability in recessionary environments.

Section 5: Value Investing Principles

The Foundation of Value Investing

This section introduces the principles of value investing as a strategic approach during recessions. Readers will explore the concept of buying undervalued assets, focusing on fundamentals, and adopting a long-term perspective to capitalize on market inefficiencies.

Contrarian Investing Strategies

Building on the discussion of value investing, this subsection explores contrarian strategies. Readers will gain insights into how contrarian investors identify opportunities by going against market trends, recognizing when assets are oversold, and positioning themselves for potential rebounds.

Section 6: Opportunistic Investing in Distressed Assets

Identifying Distressed Opportunities

This section introduces the concept of opportunistic investing in distressed assets. Readers will explore strategies for identifying undervalued opportunities during economic downturns, including distressed stocks, bonds, and real estate.

Navigating Market Panics for Long-Term Gains

Building on the discussion of opportunistic investing, this subsection delves into navigating market panics for long-term gains. Readers will gain insights into how successful investors capitalize on market dislocations, recognizing that periods of distress can create opportunities for substantial returns.

Section 7: Technology and Innovation Investments

The Resilience of Technology Stocks

This section explores the resilience of technology and innovation investments during recessions. Readers will gain insights into how certain technology stocks and innovative sectors may weather economic downturns, driven by societal shifts and advancements in digital transformation.

Balancing Growth and Stability

Building on the discussion of technology investments, this subsection emphasizes the importance of balancing growth and stability within a recession-resilient portfolio. Readers will explore strategies for integrating technology and innovation investments while managing associated risks.

Section 8: Sustainable and ESG Investing

The Rise of Sustainable Investing

This section introduces sustainable and Environmental, Social, and Governance (ESG) investing as a strategic approach during recessions.

Readers will explore how aligning investments with ethical and sustainability principles can contribute to long-term financial success.

Investing with a Purpose

Building on the discussion of sustainable investing, this subsection explores the concept of investing with a purpose. Readers will gain insights into how investments aligned with social and environmental goals can create both financial returns and positive societal impact.

Section 9: Behavioral Strategies for Volatile Markets

Harnessing Behavioral Finance

This section delves into behavioral strategies tailored for volatile markets. Readers will explore concepts from behavioral finance, such as dollar-cost averaging, rebalancing, and disciplined decision-making, designed to mitigate the impact of emotional biases during recessions.

Systematic Investment Plans and Dollar-Cost Averaging

Building on the discussion of behavioral strategies, this subsection explores the benefits of systematic investment plans and dollar-cost averaging. Readers will gain insights into how these disciplined approaches can smooth out the impact of market volatility and reduce the risk of making impulsive investment decisions.

Section 10: Risk Management in Uncertain Times

The Crucial Role of Risk Management

This section emphasizes the crucial role of risk management in recession-resilient investing. Readers will explore comprehensive risk management strategies, including diversification, stop-loss orders, and scenario analysis, designed to protect portfolios during economic downturns.

Stress Testing Portfolios

Building on the discussion of risk management, this subsection introduces the concept of stress testing portfolios. Readers will gain insights into how stress testing can assess the resilience of portfolios under extreme scenarios, enabling investors to make informed decisions to safeguard their investments.

Section 11: Investment Horizon and Long-Term Planning

The Significance of Investment Horizon

This section explores the significance of maintaining a long-term investment horizon during recessions. Readers will gain insights into how a focus on long-term goals can help investors weather short-term market fluctuations and capitalize on the power of compounding over time.

Long-Term Planning Strategies

Building on the discussion of investment horizon, this subsection provides long-term planning strategies for recession-resilient investing. Readers will explore concepts such as retirement planning, education funding, and generational wealth transfer, ensuring that investment strategies align with overarching financial goals.

Section 12: Leveraging Market Trends and Sector Rotation

Identifying Market Trends

This section explores the significance of identifying and leveraging market trends during recessions. Readers will gain insights into how recognizing emerging trends and understanding sector rotation can inform strategic investment decisions.

Sector Rotation Strategies

Building on the discussion of market trends, this subsection delves into sector rotation strategies. Readers will explore how adjusting portfolio allocations based on the relative strength of different sectors can enhance returns and manage risks in response to changing economic conditions.

Section 13: Managing Debt and Liquidity

The Impact of Debt in Recessions

This section addresses the impact of debt on investment portfolios during recessions. Readers will gain insights into managing and reducing debt levels to enhance financial resilience, particularly in times of economic uncertainty.

Leveraging Liquidity for Opportunities

Building on the discussion of debt, this subsection explores the role of liquidity in recession-resilient investing. Readers will explore strategies for maintaining adequate liquidity, positioning themselves to capitalize on investment opportunities that may arise during market downturns.

Section 14: Tactical Strategies for Market Volatility

Active vs. Passive Investing Approaches

This section introduces the debate between active and passive investing approaches during market volatility. Readers will explore the advantages and disadvantages of each approach, understanding how active strategies may be better suited to navigate recessionary environments.

Tactical Allocation Strategies

Building on the discussion of active investing, this subsection explores tactical allocation strategies. Readers will gain insights into how actively adjusting portfolio allocations based on short-term market conditions can enhance returns and manage risks in response to evolving economic landscapes.

Section 15: Investment in Precious Metals and Tangible Assets

The Role of Precious Metals

This section explores the role of precious metals, such as gold and silver, as alternative investments during recessions. Readers will gain insights into how these assets can act as a hedge against inflation and currency devaluation, adding diversification to portfolios.

Diversifying with Tangible Assets

Building on the discussion of precious metals, this subsection introduces the concept of diversifying portfolios with tangible assets. Readers will explore investments in real assets like real estate and commodities, leveraging their potential to provide stability and long-term growth.

Section 16: Global Diversification Strategies

The Importance of Global Diversification

This section emphasizes the importance of global diversification in recession-resilient portfolios. Readers will gain insights into how allocating investments across diverse geographic regions can reduce risk, enhance returns, and capture opportunities in different market conditions.

Currency Hedging and Global Opportunities

Building on the discussion of global diversification, this subsection explores the nuances of currency hedging and seizing global investment opportunities. Readers will explore strategies for managing currency risk while leveraging the potential returns offered by international markets.

Section 17: The Role of Financial Advisors in Turbulent Times

Collaborating with Financial Advisors

This section highlights the role of financial advisors in guiding investors through turbulent economic times. Readers will gain insights into the collaborative relationship between investors and advisors, understanding how professional guidance can contribute to informed decision-making.

Customizing Strategies with Advisors

Building on the discussion of financial advisors, this subsection explores the customization of investment strategies through collaborative efforts. Readers will learn how working closely with advisors allows for personalized approaches that align with individual financial goals and risk tolerances.

Section 18: Navigating Regulatory Changes and Policy Impacts

Understanding Regulatory Environments

This section addresses the impact of regulatory changes on investment strategies during recessions. Readers will gain insights into how shifts in regulations and government policies can influence market dynamics, requiring investors to adapt and navigate changing landscapes.

Adapting Strategies to Policy Changes

Building on the discussion of regulatory impacts, this subsection explores strategies for adapting to policy changes. Readers will gain insights into how staying informed about regulatory environments allows investors to proactively adjust their strategies and position themselves for success.

Section 19: Case Studies: Successful Implementation of Strategies

Real-Life Examples of Strategic Success

This section presents case studies of successful implementation of recession-resilient investment strategies. Readers will gain practical insights into how individuals and institutions navigated economic downturns, showcasing the real-world application of the strategies discussed throughout the chapter.

Key Takeaways from Case Studies

Building on the case studies, this subsection distills key takeaways and lessons learned from successful implementations of recession-resilient strategies. Readers will gain actionable insights and best practices based on the experiences of investors who effectively weathered economic challenges.

Section 20: Adapting Strategies to Post-Recession Opportunities

Transitioning to Post-Recession Environments

This section explores the transition from recessionary periods to post-recession opportunities. Readers will gain insights into adapting investment strategies as economic conditions improve, positioning portfolios for growth and capitalizing on emerging trends.

Seizing Opportunities in Recovery

Building on the discussion of post-recession environments, this subsection delves into strategies for seizing opportunities in recovery. Readers will explore how identifying emerging trends, reallocating assets, and staying agile can contribute to long-term success in dynamic market conditions.

Section 21: Conclusion - Empowering Investors for Success

Synthesizing Key Strategies

This concluding section synthesizes key strategies discussed throughout the chapter, offering readers a comprehensive overview of recession-resilient investment approaches. Key concepts such as strategic asset allocation, defensive strategies, and proactive investing are highlighted.

Encouraging Implementation and Adaptability

The chapter concludes with a call to action, encouraging readers to implement and adapt these strategies based on their unique financial goals and risk tolerances. By leveraging a diverse set of recession-resilient strategies, investors can empower themselves for success in dynamic and uncertain economic landscapes.

Chapter 8: Risk Management

Section 1: Introduction to Risk Management

Defining Risk in Investing

This section establishes the foundational concepts of risk in investing. Readers will gain a comprehensive understanding of the various forms of risk, including market risk, credit risk, and liquidity risk, laying the groundwork for effective risk management strategies.

The Importance of Risk Management

Building on the discussion of risk, this subsection emphasizes why risk management is a critical component of successful investing. Readers will explore how a proactive approach to identifying, assessing, and mitigating risks can enhance portfolio resilience and protect long-term financial goals.

Section 2: Identifying and Categorizing Risks

Systematic vs. Unsystematic Risks

This section introduces the distinction between systematic and unsystematic risks. Readers will gain insights into how systematic risks affect the entire market, while unsystematic risks are specific to individual assets. Understanding these categories is essential for tailoring risk management strategies.

Categorizing Financial Risks

Building on the discussion of systematic and unsystematic risks, this subsection delves into categorizing financial risks further. Readers will explore market risk, credit risk, operational risk, and geopolitical risk, among others, understanding the unique characteristics and challenges associated with each.

Section 3: Measuring and Assessing Risks

Quantitative and Qualitative Risk Assessment

This section introduces readers to both quantitative and qualitative approaches to risk assessment. Readers will gain insights into statistical measures, stress testing, and scenario analysis, as well as the importance of qualitative judgment in assessing risks beyond numerical metrics.

Volatility as an Indicator

Building on the discussion of risk assessment, this subsection explores the use of volatility as a key indicator. Readers will learn how volatility measures, such as standard deviation, can provide insights into the level of uncertainty and potential risks associated with different investments.

Section 4: Portfolio Diversification

The Role of Diversification in Risk Management

This section highlights the fundamental principle of portfolio diversification as a key risk management strategy. Readers will explore how spreading investments across different asset classes, industries, and geographic regions can mitigate specific risks and enhance overall portfolio stability.

Optimizing Diversification Strategies

Building on the discussion of diversification, this subsection explores optimization strategies. Readers will learn how to assess the effectiveness of diversification by considering correlations between assets, identifying optimal weightings, and adapting strategies to changing market conditions.

Section 5: Risk-Adjusted Return Metrics

Introduction to Risk-Adjusted Returns

This section introduces readers to risk-adjusted return metrics, which assess investment performance relative to the level of risk undertaken. Readers will gain insights into popular measures such as the Sharpe ratio and the information ratio, providing a holistic view of risk and return.

Evaluating Investment Efficiency

Building on the discussion of risk-adjusted returns, this subsection explores how these metrics can be used to evaluate the efficiency of investment strategies. Readers will learn how to compare different investments on a risk-adjusted basis, aiding in the selection of optimal portfolio allocations.

Section 6: Active vs. Passive Risk Management

Active Risk Management Strategies

This section explores active risk management strategies, where investors actively make decisions to respond to changing market conditions. Readers will gain insights into techniques such as stop-loss orders, dynamic asset allocation, and tactical adjustments to manage risks proactively.

Passive Risk Management Approaches

Building on the discussion of active strategies, this subsection introduces passive risk management approaches. Readers will explore techniques such as strategic asset allocation and buy-and-hold strategies, understanding how these methods aim to maintain a consistent risk profile over time.

Section 7: Hedging Strategies for Risk Mitigation

The Role of Hedging in Risk Management

This section explores the concept of hedging as a specific strategy for mitigating risks. Readers will gain insights into how derivative instruments, such as options and futures contracts, can be used to protect portfolios against adverse market movements.

Tailoring Hedging Strategies

Building on the discussion of hedging, this subsection delves into tailoring hedging strategies based on specific risk exposures. Readers will learn how to identify areas of vulnerability within their portfolios and implement targeted hedging strategies to address those particular risks.

Section 8: Stress Testing and Scenario Analysis

The Importance of Stress Testing

This section emphasizes the importance of stress testing as a proactive risk management tool. Readers will gain insights into how stress testing simulates extreme market conditions, allowing investors to assess the resilience of their portfolios and identify potential vulnerabilities.

Scenario Analysis for Informed Decision-Making

Building on the discussion of stress testing, this subsection introduces scenario analysis as a complementary tool for informed decision-making. Readers will explore how analyzing different hypothetical scenarios can enhance risk awareness and guide strategic adjustments to portfolio allocations.

Section 9: Liquidity Risk Management

Understanding Liquidity Risk

This section explores the unique challenges posed by liquidity risk and its potential impact on investment portfolios. Readers will gain insights into how insufficient liquidity can lead to increased trading costs, price slippage, and difficulties in executing desired investment strategies.

Strategies for Managing Liquidity Risk

Building on the discussion of liquidity risk, this subsection delves into strategies for managing and mitigating liquidity challenges. Readers will learn how to assess the liquidity of assets, implement liquidity risk controls, and incorporate liquidity considerations into overall risk management frameworks.

Section 10: Behavioral Aspects of Risk Management

The Influence of Behavioral Biases

This section addresses the behavioral aspects of risk management, recognizing the impact of cognitive biases on decision-making. Readers will gain insights into common biases such as loss aversion, overconfidence, and herding, understanding how these biases can affect risk perceptions and actions.

Strategies for Overcoming Behavioral Biases

Building on the discussion of behavioral biases, this subsection introduces strategies for overcoming these inherent cognitive challenges. Readers will learn how to cultivate self-awareness, implement decision-making frameworks, and leverage diversification to counteract the influence of behavioral biases.

Section 11: Cybersecurity and Operational Risk

Recognizing Operational Risks

This section explores the importance of recognizing and managing operational risks, including those related to cybersecurity threats. Readers will gain insights into the potential consequences of operational failures and the importance of implementing robust cybersecurity measures.

Building Resilience Against Operational Risks

Building on the discussion of operational risks, this subsection delves into strategies for building resilience against cybersecurity threats and other operational challenges. Readers will learn how proactive measures, employee training, and technology safeguards contribute to overall risk mitigation.

Section 12: Compliance and Regulatory Risk

Navigating Compliance Challenges

This section addresses the challenges posed by compliance and regulatory risks. Readers will gain insights into the importance of staying informed about regulatory changes, maintaining compliance with industry standards, and implementing effective risk management practices to navigate evolving regulatory environments.

Incorporating Regulatory Considerations into Risk Management

Building on the discussion of regulatory risks, this subsection explores strategies for incorporating regulatory considerations into overall risk management frameworks. Readers will learn how proactive compliance measures can enhance portfolio resilience and protect against legal and regulatory challenges.

Section 13: Environmental, Social, and Governance (ESG) Considerations

Recognizing ESG Risks

This section introduces readers to the considerations of environmental, social, and governance (ESG) risks. Readers will explore how factors such as climate change, social responsibility, and corporate governance can pose risks and opportunities for investors.

Integrating ESG Principles into Risk Management

Building on the discussion of ESG risks, this subsection delves into strategies for integrating ESG principles into overall risk management frameworks. Readers will learn how aligning investments with ESG criteria can contribute to long-term sustainability and risk mitigation.

Section 14: Case Studies: Effective Risk Management in Action

Real-Life Examples of Risk Mitigation

This section presents case studies highlighting effective risk management practices in real-world scenarios. Readers will gain practical insights into how individuals and institutions successfully identified, assessed, and mitigated risks, showcasing the application of risk management principles.

Key Takeaways from Risk Management Case Studies

Building on the case studies, this subsection distills key takeaways and lessons learned from successful risk management implementations. Readers will gain actionable insights and best practices based on the experiences of investors who effectively navigated complex risk landscapes.

Section 15: Preparing for the Unexpected

The Unpredictability of Risks

This section emphasizes the unpredictable nature of risks and the importance of preparing for the unexpected. Readers will explore the concept of black swan events and the need for adaptable risk management strategies that can respond to unforeseen challenges.

Building Resilience for Long-Term Success

Building on the discussion of unpredictability, this subsection explores strategies for building resilience to withstand unexpected risks. Readers will learn how cultivating a dynamic risk management approach, staying informed, and continuously adapting strategies contribute to long-term investment success.

Section 16: Emerging Risks in the Modern Landscape

Identifying New Challenges

This section explores emerging risks in the modern investment landscape. Readers will gain insights into challenges posed by technological advancements, global interconnectedness, and other factors that introduce new dimensions to risk management.

Anticipating Technological Disruptions

Building on the discussion of emerging risks, this subsection delves into the impact of technological disruptions. Readers will explore the challenges and opportunities presented by innovations such as artificial intelligence, blockchain, and other technological advancements, emphasizing the need for proactive risk management.

Section 17: Behavioral Finance in Risk Management

Applying Behavioral Insights

This section applies principles from behavioral finance specifically to the realm of risk management. Readers will explore how understanding behavioral biases can inform more effective risk management strategies, helping investors navigate emotional challenges and make rational decisions in the face of uncertainty.

The Role of Decision Heuristics

Building on the discussion of behavioral finance, this subsection explores decision heuristics and their influence on risk management. Readers will gain insights into how mental shortcuts and cognitive biases impact decision-making processes, and strategies for mitigating their effects on risk assessments.

Section 18: Dynamic Risk Models for Adaptive Strategies

The Need for Dynamic Models

This section highlights the importance of dynamic risk models that can adapt to changing market conditions. Readers will gain insights into the limitations of static risk models and the benefits of incorporating flexibility and adaptability into risk management frameworks.

Implementing Dynamic Risk Assessments

Building on the discussion of dynamic models, this subsection explores practical ways to implement dynamic risk assessments. Readers will learn how to integrate real-time data, market indicators, and scenario planning into risk management practices, allowing for more responsive and agile decision-making.

Section 19: Regulatory Compliance and Ethical Considerations

The Evolving Regulatory Landscape

This section addresses the evolving regulatory landscape and its impact on risk management practices. Readers will gain insights into the importance of staying abreast of regulatory changes, ensuring compliance, and upholding ethical standards in risk management.

Balancing Compliance and Ethical Decision-Making

Building on the discussion of regulatory compliance, this subsection explores the delicate balance between adhering to regulations and making ethically sound decisions. Readers will learn how ethical considerations should be woven into risk management strategies to foster long-term trust and sustainability.

Section 20: Integrated Risk Management for Holistic Approaches

The Holistic Nature of Risks

This section emphasizes the holistic nature of risks, advocating for integrated risk management approaches that consider a wide range of factors. Readers will gain insights into how risks are interconnected, and how addressing them comprehensively contributes to overall portfolio resilience.

Integrating Environmental, Social, and Governance (ESG) Factors

Building on the discussion of holistic approaches, this subsection explores the integration of ESG factors into risk management. Readers will learn how considering environmental, social, and governance criteria can provide a more nuanced understanding of risks and enhance long-term sustainability.

Section 21: Case Studies: Lessons Learned from Risk Management Challenges

Real-Life Challenges and Solutions

This section presents case studies that showcase real-life challenges in risk management and the corresponding solutions implemented. Readers will gain practical insights into navigating complex risk scenarios, learning from the experiences of individuals and institutions that effectively managed and mitigated risks.

Extracting Practical Insights

Building on the case studies, this subsection distills practical insights and lessons learned from the challenges presented. Readers will gain actionable takeaways and best practices to enhance their risk management strategies, ensuring a proactive and resilient approach to potential risks.

Section 22: The Continuous Evolution of Risk Management

Acknowledging the Dynamic Nature of Risks

This section acknowledges the continuous evolution of risks and risk management practices. Readers will gain insights into the need for ongoing education, adaptability, and a forward-looking mindset to navigate the ever-changing landscape of investment risks.

The Role of Technological Advancements

Building on the discussion of continuous evolution, this subsection explores the role of technological advancements in reshaping risk management. Readers will learn about innovative tools, analytics, and technologies that can enhance risk assessment and decision-making in the modern era.

Section 23: Empowering Investors through Risk Literacy

Promoting Risk Literacy

This section advocates for the importance of risk literacy among investors. Readers will explore the concept of risk literacy—understanding, assessing, and managing risks effectively—and its role in empowering investors to make informed decisions and navigate turbulent markets.

Tools for Enhancing Risk Literacy

Building on the discussion of risk literacy, this subsection introduces practical tools and resources for investors to enhance their understanding of risks. Readers will learn about risk assessment frameworks, educational platforms, and industry resources that contribute to building a robust risk-aware mindset.

Section 24: Conclusion - Building Resilient Portfolios through Effective Risk Management

Synthesizing Key Risk Management Principles

This concluding section synthesizes key risk management principles discussed throughout the chapter. Readers are reminded of the importance of proactive risk management in building resilient portfolios and safeguarding long-term financial goals.

Encouraging a Proactive and Adaptive Mindset

The chapter concludes with a call to action, encouraging readers to adopt a proactive and adaptive mindset in their risk management practices. By staying informed, embracing innovation, and integrating ethical considerations, investors can navigate risks effectively and position themselves for sustained success.

Chapter 9: Case Studies: Successful Investments

Section 1: Introduction to Real-Life Success Stories

Unveiling the Power of Resilient Investments

In this section, we delve into the world of real-life success stories during economic downturns. Readers will embark on a journey through diverse case studies that showcase how savvy investors navigated turbulent times, made strategic decisions, and turned challenges into opportunities.

The Inspirational Role of Case Studies

Building on the introduction, this subsection underscores the inspirational role of case studies. By exploring the triumphs and trials of investors who weathered economic storms, readers can gain valuable insights, draw inspiration, and extract practical lessons to apply in their own investment journeys.

Section 2: The Early 1990s Recession (1990-1991): A Lesson in Prudent Decision-Making

Background of the Early 1990s Recession

This section sets the stage by revisiting the Early 1990s Recession, a downturn characterized by the savings and loan crisis, high-interest rates, and a slowdown in consumer spending. Readers will gain insights into the economic backdrop that influenced investment decisions during this period.

Case Study 1: Strategic Real Estate Investments

The first case study explores how shrewd investors capitalized on distressed real estate opportunities during the Early 1990s Recession. By strategically acquiring undervalued properties, these investors not only navigated the downturn but also positioned themselves for substantial returns as the real estate market rebounded.

Case Study 2: Diversification Beyond Traditional Assets

Building on the real estate success, this subsection explores how some investors diversified beyond traditional asset classes. By incorporating alternative investments such as precious metals and unconventional assets, these individuals mitigated risks and achieved a well-rounded portfolio that thrived amid economic uncertainties.

Section 3: The Dot-Com Bubble Burst (2000-2001): Navigating the Tech Wreck

Background of the Dot-Com Bubble Burst

This section revisits the Dot-Com Bubble Burst, a period marked by the collapse of many internet-based companies and a decline in the stock market. Readers will gain insights into the unique challenges posed by the burst of the tech bubble and its ripple effects on the broader economy.

Case Study 3: Contrarian Investing in Tech

The third case study examines investors who adopted a contrarian approach during the Dot-Com Bubble Burst. By identifying oversold technology stocks with strong fundamentals, these contrarian investors positioned themselves for substantial gains when the market eventually rebounded, showcasing the power of strategic contrarianism.

Case Study 4: Embracing Innovation in Adversity

Building on the contrarian success, this subsection explores how some investors embraced innovation amidst the tech wreck. By identifying disruptive technologies and investing in companies with transformative visions, these individuals not only navigated the downturn but also participated in the subsequent tech-driven economic recovery.

Section 4: The Global Financial Crisis (2007-2009): Lessons from Market Meltdown

Background of the Global Financial Crisis

This section revisits the Global Financial Crisis triggered by the collapse of the housing bubble. Readers will gain insights into the widespread economic downturn, the banking failures, and the intricate factors that led to one of the most severe financial crises in modern history.

Case Study 5: Opportunistic Real Estate Investments

The fifth case study explores how savvy investors seized opportunities in the distressed real estate market during the Global Financial Crisis. By acquiring foreclosed properties and distressed assets at discounted prices, these investors not only navigated the crisis but also positioned themselves for lucrative returns as the real estate market rebounded.

Case Study 6: Defensive Strategies and Dividend Stocks

Building on the real estate success, this subsection delves into the defensive strategies employed by some investors during the crisis. By shifting focus to stable, dividend-paying stocks and defensive sectors, these individuals managed to weather the storm and generate consistent income amid market turmoil.

Section 5: The Eurozone Crisis (2009-2013): Navigating Sovereign Debt Challenges

Background of the Eurozone Crisis

This section revisits the Eurozone Crisis, focusing on sovereign debt issues and banking failures that affected countries such as Greece, Portugal, Ireland, Italy, and Spain. Readers will gain insights into the complexities of this crisis and its impact on the European economy.

Case Study 7: Global Diversification and Currency Hedging

The seventh case study explores how investors embraced global diversification and currency hedging strategies during the Eurozone Crisis. By allocating investments across diverse geographic regions and implementing currency hedging techniques, these individuals mitigated risks and achieved stability in their portfolios.

Case Study 8: Sustainable Investments in Challenging Environments

Building on the global diversification success, this subsection explores how some investors integrated sustainable and ESG principles into their portfolios. By aligning investments with environmental, social, and governance considerations, these individuals not only navigated the crisis but also contributed to positive societal and environmental impact.

Section 6: The Great Depression (1929-1939): Endurance and Long-Term Vision

Background of the Great Depression

This section revisits the Great Depression, the most severe worldwide economic downturn in the 20th century. Readers will gain insights into the widespread unemployment, bank failures, and economic challenges that characterized this era.

Case Study 9: Long-Term Value Investing

The ninth case study explores the enduring success of investors who adhered to long-term value investing principles during the Great Depression. By focusing on fundamentally sound companies with strong financials, these investors not only survived the downturn but also thrived in the subsequent economic recovery.

Case Study 10: Socially Responsible Investing for Community Support

Building on the value investing success, this subsection delves into how some investors embraced socially responsible investing during the Great Depression. By supporting companies that prioritized social responsibility and community welfare, these individuals contributed to both economic recovery and societal well-being.

Section 7: The COVID-19 Pandemic Recession (2020): Resilience in Unprecedented Times

Background of the COVID-19 Pandemic Recession

This section explores the recent COVID-19 Pandemic Recession, marked by widespread lockdowns, supply chain disruptions, and a decline in consumer spending. Readers will gain insights into the unique challenges posed by the global pandemic and its impact on various sectors.

Case Study 11: Technology and Remote Work Revolution

The eleventh case study examines how investors capitalized on the technology and remote work revolution during the COVID-19 Pandemic Recession. By identifying opportunities in the technology sector and companies facilitating remote work, these investors not only navigated the crisis but also positioned themselves for sustained growth in the post-pandemic era.

Case Study 12: Healthcare and Biotech Innovations

Building on the technology success, this subsection explores how some investors embraced healthcare and biotech innovations. By identifying companies at the forefront of vaccine development, telemedicine, and medical advancements, these individuals not only contributed to pandemic response efforts but also achieved remarkable returns.

Section 8: Key Takeaways and Lessons Learned

Extracting Lessons for Thriving Investments

This section distills key takeaways and lessons learned from the diverse case studies presented throughout the chapter. Readers will gain actionable insights into resilient investment strategies, adaptability in dynamic markets, and the enduring principles that contribute to successful investment outcomes.

Navigating Uncertainty with Confidence

Building on the lessons learned, this subsection emphasizes the importance of navigating uncertainty with confidence. By embracing a diverse set of investment strategies, learning from historical successes, and remaining adaptable, investors can position themselves to thrive in dynamic and unpredictable economic landscapes.

Chapter 10: Preparing for the Aftermath

Section 1: Introduction - Anticipating Recovery and Opportunities

Setting the Stage for Post-Recession Perspectives

In this introductory section, we explore the anticipation of economic recovery and opportunities that follow a recession. Readers are encouraged to shift their focus from crisis management to strategic planning, laying the groundwork for the insights and strategies to be unveiled in subsequent sections.

The Dynamics of Post-Recession Environments

Building on the introduction, this subsection delves into the dynamics of post-recession environments. By understanding the unique characteristics of recovery phases, readers can gain insights into how economic landscapes transform and identify potential avenues for growth and prosperity.

Section 2: Identifying Post-Recession Opportunities

Economic Recovery Patterns

This section examines different economic recovery patterns, from V-shaped recoveries characterized by rapid rebound to U-shaped and W-shaped patterns indicating a more prolonged recovery. Readers will gain insights into how these patterns influence investment strategies and decision-making in the aftermath of a recession.

Case Study 1: The 2008 Financial Crisis Recovery

The first case study analyzes the recovery following the 2008 financial crisis, providing insights into the challenges and opportunities that arose during the post-recession period. Readers will gain a nuanced understanding of the factors that shaped the recovery trajectory and the investment strategies that proved successful.

Identifying Sectors Poised for Growth

Building on recovery patterns, this subsection explores how investors can identify sectors poised for growth in the aftermath of a recession. By examining historical examples and market dynamics, readers will gain insights into sectors that tend to outperform during recovery phases, guiding strategic investment decisions.

Section 3: Investment Strategies for Post-Recession Success

Tactical Asset Allocation

This section introduces readers to tactical asset allocation strategies tailored for post-recession environments. By dynamically adjusting portfolio allocations based on evolving market conditions, investors can capitalize on emerging opportunities and navigate uncertainties with agility.

Case Study 2: Navigating the Post-Dot-Com Bubble Recovery

The second case study explores how investors navigated the post-Dot-Com Bubble recovery, emphasizing the role of tactical asset allocation in optimizing portfolio performance. Readers will gain practical insights into how strategic adjustments contributed to success in the aftermath of the tech-driven downturn.

Strategic Stock Picking and Value Investing

Building on tactical asset allocation, this subsection delves into the merits of strategic stock picking and value investing in post-recession scenarios. By identifying undervalued stocks with strong fundamentals, investors can position themselves for potential long-term growth and capitalize on market inefficiencies.

Section 4: Real Estate Opportunities in Post-Recession Periods

Property Market Dynamics

This section explores the dynamics of the real estate market in the aftermath of a recession. Readers will gain insights into how economic recovery influences property values, rental markets, and investment opportunities, shaping strategic decisions for real estate investors.

Case Study 3: Post-Global Financial Crisis Real Estate Rebound

The third case study examines the real estate rebound following the Global Financial Crisis, highlighting successful investment strategies. Readers will learn from investors who capitalized on distressed properties, navigated changing rental markets, and achieved substantial returns during the recovery.

Commercial Real Estate and Innovative Models

Building on real estate dynamics, this subsection explores opportunities in commercial real estate and innovative investment models. From office spaces to logistics hubs, readers will gain insights into emerging trends and strategies for tapping into the potential of the commercial real estate sector in post-recession landscapes.

Section 5: Entrepreneurship and Business Opportunities

Seizing Entrepreneurial Opportunities

This section encourages readers to consider entrepreneurship as a viable avenue for post-recession success. By exploring case studies and examples of successful businesses born during economic recoveries, readers can gain inspiration and insights into the entrepreneurial landscape.

Case Study 4: Startups That Thrived Post-Digital Revolution

The fourth case study examines startups that thrived in the aftermath of the Digital Revolution. Readers will learn from the strategies adopted by these entrepreneurial ventures, how they identified emerging market needs, and positioned themselves for sustained success in a rapidly evolving business landscape.

Innovation and Adaptation in Business Models

Building on entrepreneurial opportunities, this subsection explores the importance of innovation and adaptation in business models. Readers will gain insights into how businesses that embrace change, adopt cutting-edge technologies, and cater to evolving consumer preferences can thrive in the post-recession period.

Section 6: Global Perspectives on Post-Recession Opportunities

Analyzing Global Economic Trends

This section analyzes global economic trends and their impact on post-recession opportunities. Readers will gain insights into the interconnected nature of economies, how global trends shape recovery trajectories, and the potential for cross-border investment strategies.

Case Study 5: Emerging Markets and Post-Crisis Growth

The fifth case study explores opportunities in emerging markets during post-crisis periods. Readers will learn from investors who successfully navigated risks and capitalized on the growth potential of emerging economies, providing a broader perspective on global investment strategies.

Currency Considerations and Foreign Exchange Markets

Building on global economic trends, this subsection delves into currency considerations and the role of foreign exchange markets in post-recession investment strategies. Readers will gain insights into how currency dynamics can influence returns and how strategic positioning in forex markets can enhance overall portfolio performance.

Section 7: Sustainable Investing for Long-Term Growth

The Rise of Sustainable Investing

This section explores the rise of sustainable investing and its relevance in post-recession environments. Readers will gain insights into how environmental, social, and governance (ESG) considerations can align with long-term growth objectives and contribute to resilient and ethical investment portfolios.

Case Study 6: Companies that Thrived Through Sustainable Practices

The sixth case study examines companies that thrived by prioritizing sustainable practices during the post-recession period. Readers will learn from businesses that integrated ESG principles into their operations, attracting conscientious investors and positioning themselves for long-term success.

Investing in Green Technologies and Renewable Energy

Building on sustainable investing, this subsection explores opportunities in green technologies and renewable energy. Readers will gain insights into the growing importance of environmentally conscious investments and how supporting innovations in clean energy can align with both financial and ethical objectives.

Section 8: The Role of Technology in Post-Recession Strategies

Technology as an Enabler of Growth

This section emphasizes the transformative role of technology in post-recession strategies. Readers will gain insights into how technological advancements can drive innovation, reshape industries, and present new opportunities for investors seeking growth in a rapidly evolving digital landscape.

Case Study 7: Tech Giants that Emerged Stronger Post-Recession

The seventh case study examines technology giants that emerged stronger in the aftermath of economic downturns. Readers will learn from the strategies employed by these companies, how they navigated challenges, and capitalized on the digital transformation to achieve sustained success.

Investing in Disruptive Technologies and Emerging Trends

Building on the role of technology, this subsection explores the potential of investing in disruptive technologies and emerging trends. From artificial intelligence to biotechnology, readers will gain insights into how staying at the forefront of technological advancements can drive post-recession investment success.

Section 9: Financial Planning and Wealth Preservation

Securing Financial Stability

This section focuses on financial planning strategies to secure stability and wealth preservation in post-recession periods. Readers will gain insights into risk management, debt reduction, and investment strategies that contribute to building a robust financial foundation for the long term.

Case Study 8: Wealth Preservation Strategies Post-Eurozone Crisis

The eighth case study examines wealth preservation strategies adopted by investors in the aftermath of the Eurozone Crisis. Readers will learn from individuals who safeguarded their wealth through strategic financial planning, providing practical insights into preserving financial well-being during uncertainties.

Retirement Planning and Long-Term Financial Goals

Building on financial planning, this subsection explores the importance of retirement planning and setting long-term financial goals. Readers will gain insights into how strategic financial decisions made during the post-recession period can contribute to a secure and comfortable retirement.

Section 10: Expert Insights on Post-Recession Strategies

Gathering Perspectives from Seasoned Investors

This section gathers insights from seasoned investors and financial experts on post-recession strategies. Readers will benefit from a diverse range of perspectives, strategies, and recommendations, providing a well-rounded understanding of how experienced professionals approach investment opportunities in the aftermath of economic downturns.

Case Study 9: Lessons from Renowned Investors

The ninth case study delves into the lessons learned from renowned investors who navigated multiple post-recession periods successfully. Readers will gain wisdom from the experiences of these financial stalwarts, offering valuable guidance for their own investment journeys.

Section 11: Mitigating Risks in the Post-Recession Landscape

Recognizing and Managing New Risks

This section explores the risks that may emerge in the post-recession landscape and strategies for recognizing and managing them. Readers will gain insights into potential pitfalls, uncertainties, and proactive measures to safeguard their investments in a recovering economic environment.

Case Study 10: Navigating Unforeseen Challenges Post-COVID-19

The tenth case study examines how investors navigated unforeseen challenges in the post-COVID-19 landscape. Readers will learn from individuals who successfully adapted their strategies to address unexpected risks, providing valuable lessons for anticipating and mitigating uncertainties.

Section 12: Preparing for the Next Economic Cycle

The Cyclical Nature of Economies

This section underscores the cyclical nature of economies and the inevitability of future economic cycles. Readers will gain insights into the importance of adopting forward-looking strategies that position them not only for current recovery but also for future downturns and subsequent upswings.

Case Study 11: Strategies for Prolonged Economic Stability

The eleventh case study explores strategies adopted by investors for prolonged economic stability. Readers will learn from individuals who not only thrived in the post-recession period but also positioned themselves strategically to weather potential future economic challenges.

Section 13: Conclusion - A Roadmap for Post-Recession Success

Synthesizing Key Insights and Strategies

This concluding section synthesizes key insights and strategies presented throughout the chapter. Readers are provided with a comprehensive roadmap for post-recession success, incorporating diverse perspectives, case studies, and expert recommendations.

Encouraging Proactive and Informed Decision-Making

The chapter concludes with a call to action, encouraging readers to embrace proactive and informed decision-making in the aftermath of recessions. By leveraging the insights gained, staying adaptable, and adopting a strategic mindset, investors can position themselves to not only survive but thrive in the evolving economic landscape.

Chapter 11: Expert Insights

Section 1: Introduction - Wisdom from the Pros

Setting the Stage for Expert Perspectives

In this introductory section, we explore the invaluable insights that seasoned investors and financial experts bring to the table. Readers are introduced to the wealth of knowledge that can be gained by tapping into the experiences and wisdom of those who have navigated multiple economic cycles.

The Significance of Expert Perspectives

Building on the introduction, this subsection underscores the significance of expert perspectives. By delving into the thought processes, strategies, and lessons learned from experienced professionals, readers can enhance their understanding of investment dynamics and gain a more nuanced view of navigating uncertainties.

Section 2: Gathering Perspectives from Renowned Investors

Insights from Investment Titans

This section features insights from renowned investors who have weathered various economic storms. Readers will benefit from the experiences of financial stalwarts, gaining wisdom on investment strategies, risk management, and maintaining resilience in the face of market challenges.

Case Study 1: Warren Buffett - The Oracle of Omaha

The first case study delves into the investment philosophy of Warren Buffett. Readers will gain insights into Buffett's long-term value investing approach, principles for evaluating companies, and how he navigated economic downturns to build one of the most successful investment portfolios in history.

Case Study 2: Ray Dalio - Bridgewater Associates

The second case study explores the principles of Ray Dalio, founder of Bridgewater Associates. Readers will learn from Dalio's perspectives on economic cycles, the importance of diversification, and his unique approach to managing risks during periods of financial turbulence.

Case Study 3: Peter Lynch - Magellan Fund

The third case study examines the investment strategies of Peter Lynch during his tenure at the Magellan Fund. Readers will gain insights into Lynch's approach to identifying growth opportunities, the significance of thorough research, and adapting to evolving market conditions.

Section 3: Lessons from Seasoned Financial Advisors

Guidance from Financial Planning Experts

This section features insights from seasoned financial advisors who have guided clients through various economic climates. Readers will gain perspectives on financial planning, wealth management, and strategies for building resilient portfolios.

Case Study 4: Suze Orman - Personal Finance Guru

The fourth case study explores the advice of Suze Orman, a renowned personal finance expert. Readers will learn from Orman's principles on budgeting, debt management, and long-term financial planning, providing actionable insights for securing financial stability.

Case Study 5: David Swensen - Yale Endowment Model

The fifth case study delves into the investment model of David Swensen, the long-time chief investment officer of Yale University's endowment. Readers will gain insights into Swensen's approach to portfolio diversification, alternative investments, and managing institutional funds for consistent returns.

Section 4: Strategies from Institutional Investors

Navigating Complex Portfolios

This section explores strategies employed by institutional investors to navigate complex and large-scale portfolios. Readers will gain insights into the decision-making processes of organizations managing substantial assets, providing a different perspective from individual investors.

Case Study 6: Harvard Management Company - Endowment Strategies

The sixth case study examines the endowment strategies of Harvard Management Company. Readers will learn from the institution's approach to asset allocation, diversification across different asset classes, and the challenges and opportunities faced in managing a large endowment.

Case Study 7: Pension Fund Strategies for Long-Term Growth

The seventh case study explores the investment strategies of pension funds focused on achieving long-term growth. Readers will gain insights into how pension funds balance risk and return, manage liabilities, and adapt their investment approaches to changing economic landscapes.

Section 5: Perspectives from Economic Analysts and Forecasters

Analyzing Economic Trends

This section features insights from economic analysts and forecasters who specialize in interpreting economic trends. Readers will gain a better understanding of the factors influencing global economies and how to interpret forecasts for informed investment decisions.

Case Study 8: Insights from Leading Economists

The eighth case study gathers insights from leading economists on current economic trends and future projections. Readers will gain perspectives on global economic dynamics, potential challenges, and areas of opportunity for investors in the coming years.

Case Study 9: Financial Journalists' Perspectives on Market Trends

The ninth case study explores the perspectives of financial journalists reporting on market trends. Readers will gain insights into how journalists analyze financial news, interpret economic data, and provide context for investors navigating a rapidly changing information landscape.

Section 6: Adaptability and Innovation in Investment Strategies

Embracing Change in Investment Approaches

This section explores the importance of adaptability and innovation in contemporary investment strategies. Readers will gain insights into how successful investors continually evolve their approaches to meet the challenges and opportunities presented by dynamic markets.

Case Study 10: Innovations in Quantitative Investing

The tenth case study delves into innovations in quantitative investing and algorithmic trading. Readers will learn how technological advancements have reshaped investment strategies, providing faster decision-making and increased efficiency in portfolio management.

Case Study 11: Fintech Disruption in the Financial Industry

The eleventh case study explores the disruptive influence of fintech in the financial industry. Readers will gain insights into how technological innovations, from robo-advisors to blockchain, are transforming traditional financial services and creating new opportunities for investors.

Section 7: Ethical and Responsible Investing Practices

Integrating Ethics into Investment Decisions

This section emphasizes the growing importance of ethical and responsible investing practices. Readers will gain insights into how investors can align their portfolios with environmental, social, and governance (ESG) considerations for long-term sustainability.

Case Study 12: Impact Investing for Positive Change

The twelfth case study explores impact investing and how investors can contribute to positive societal and environmental change. Readers will learn from examples of successful impact investing, showcasing how financial returns can be aligned with making a meaningful impact on the world.

Case Study 13: Corporate Social Responsibility and Shareholder Value

The thirteenth case study examines the relationship between corporate social responsibility (CSR) and shareholder value. Readers will gain insights into how companies that prioritize ethical practices and social responsibility can create value for both investors and society.

Section 8: Navigating Regulatory Changes and Policy Impacts

Understanding the Regulatory Landscape

This section explores the impact of regulatory changes on investment strategies. Readers will gain insights into how shifts in financial regulations and government policies can influence market dynamics, presenting both challenges and opportunities for investors.

Case Study 14: Navigating Investment Strategies Amid Regulatory Changes

The fourteenth case study examines how investors successfully navigated their strategies amid regulatory changes. Readers will learn from examples of adapting to new financial regulations, managing compliance, and leveraging opportunities created by evolving policy landscapes.

Section 9: Behavioral Finance and Decision-Making

Psychology in Investment Choices

This section delves into the realm of behavioral finance and its implications for investment decision-making. Readers will gain insights into how psychological biases and emotions can impact investment choices and strategies for overcoming cognitive pitfalls.

Case Study 15: Behavioral Finance in Action

The fifteenth case study analyzes real-world scenarios where behavioral finance played a pivotal role. Readers will learn from instances where understanding investor psychology led to more informed decisions, providing practical lessons for mitigating the impact of behavioral biases.

Section 10: Global Economic Trends and Geopolitical Influences

Navigating Global Economic Shifts

This section examines the interconnectedness of global economic trends and geopolitical influences on investment strategies. Readers will gain insights into how geopolitical events, trade dynamics, and international relations can shape investment landscapes.

Case Study 16: Investments in a Changing Global Geopolitical Landscape

The sixteenth case study explores how investors adapted their strategies in response to changing global geopolitical landscapes. Readers will learn from examples of navigating uncertainties arising from geopolitical events, providing valuable insights for positioning portfolios in an interconnected world.

Section 11: Technological Innovations in Investment Management

Fintech Advancements in Investment

This section focuses on technological innovations reshaping investment management. Readers will gain insights into the role of artificial intelligence, machine learning, and big data analytics in optimizing investment processes and decision-making.

Case Study 17: The Rise of Algorithmic Trading

The seventeenth case study delves into the rise of algorithmic trading and its impact on investment strategies. Readers will learn from examples of successful algorithmic trading, understanding how technology-driven approaches can enhance trading efficiency and responsiveness.

Section 12: Sustainable Investing Beyond ESG Criteria

Evolving Perspectives on Sustainable Investing

This section explores the evolving landscape of sustainable investing beyond traditional ESG criteria. Readers will gain insights into emerging trends such as impact investing, green bonds, and other avenues for aligning investments with broader environmental and social goals.

Case Study 18: Holistic Approaches to Sustainable Investment

The eighteenth case study examines holistic approaches to sustainable investment. Readers will learn from examples of investors integrating sustainability considerations across their entire portfolios, showcasing the potential for financial returns alongside positive societal and environmental impacts.

Section 13: Risk Management Strategies for Volatile Markets

Proactive Approaches to Risk Mitigation

This section emphasizes proactive risk management strategies for navigating volatile markets. Readers will gain insights into tools, techniques, and practices employed by experts to identify, assess, and mitigate risks in dynamic and unpredictable economic environments.

Case Study 19: Successful Risk Mitigation in Unpredictable Markets

The nineteenth case study showcases instances where investors successfully mitigated risks in unpredictable markets. Readers will learn from examples of anticipating and addressing potential pitfalls, providing valuable lessons for building resilience in investment portfolios.

Section 14: Post-Pandemic Investment Strategies

Lessons from the COVID-19 Pandemic

This section reflects on the lessons learned from the COVID-19 pandemic and their implications for post-pandemic investment strategies. Readers will gain insights into how the unprecedented challenges of the pandemic have influenced investor behavior and market dynamics.

Case Study 20: Adapting Strategies Post-COVID-19

The twentieth case study examines how investors adapted their strategies in the aftermath of the COVID-19 pandemic. Readers will learn from examples of resilience, innovation, and strategic adjustments made in response to the unique challenges posed by the global health crisis.

Section 15: The Future of Investing - Emerging Trends and Paradigms

Anticipating Future Investment Landscapes

This section explores emerging trends and paradigm shifts shaping the future of investing. Readers will gain insights into how factors like sustainability, technological advancements, and societal changes are influencing the trajectory of investment landscapes.

Case Study 21: Investing in Future Megatrends

The twenty-first case study examines investments in future megatrends, showcasing how forward-thinking investors positioned themselves to capitalize on long-term shifts in demographics, technology, and global dynamics.

Section 16: Building Resilient Portfolios for Long-Term Success

The Art of Portfolio Resilience

This section synthesizes key insights from experts on building resilient portfolios for long-term success. Readers will gain a comprehensive understanding of the principles, strategies, and practices that contribute to enduring success in the ever-evolving world of investments.

Case Study 22: Resilient Portfolios in Action

The twenty-second case study provides real-world examples of resilient portfolios in action. Readers will learn from instances where diversified, adaptive, and strategically managed portfolios weathered various economic storms, offering practical lessons for crafting robust investment strategies.

Section 17: Conclusion - A Call to Informed Action

The Ongoing Journey of Investment Mastery

This concluding section emphasizes the ongoing journey of investment mastery and the importance of continuous learning and adaptation. Readers are encouraged to apply the expert insights gained throughout the chapter, shaping their investment approaches in alignment with the ever-changing dynamics of global markets.

Empowering Investors for Future Success

The chapter concludes with a call to action, empowering investors to navigate uncertainties with confidence, informed decision-making, and a forward-looking mindset. By embracing the wisdom of experts, staying attuned to evolving trends, and adapting to new paradigms, investors can position themselves for enduring success in the dynamic world of investments.

Final Chapter: Thriving in Uncertain Times

Introduction

In this concluding chapter, we synthesize the key lessons from the preceding chapters, providing readers with a comprehensive guide to navigating and thriving in uncertain economic landscapes. The journey through the chapters has been a voyage into the intricacies of recessionary periods, investment strategies, expert insights, and the evolving nature of global markets.

Chapter 1: Navigating Turbulent Times

The journey begins with the foundational understanding laid in Chapter 1, where we set the stage for investing during recessions. Recognizing the inevitability of economic downturns, we emphasized the importance of preparedness and a strategic mindset. As we conclude, the essence of this initial chapter resonates throughout the subsequent discussions, reinforcing the idea that proactive preparation is the bedrock of resilient investing.

Chapter 2: Understanding Recessions

Moving into Chapter 2, we deepened our comprehension of recessions, unraveling their intricacies and impact on the broader economy. Understanding the cyclical nature of economic downturns became a pivotal theme, highlighting the significance of historical context in shaping our approach to current and future recessions. The insights gained in this chapter serve as a lens through which we analyze the subsequent economic challenges and opportunities.

Chapter 3: Learning from the Past

In Chapter 3, we embarked on a historical exploration of significant recessions, drawing lessons from events like the Early 1990s Recession, the Dot-Com Bubble Burst, the Global Financial Crisis, the Eurozone Crisis, the Great Depression, and the Post-World War II

Recession. These historical case studies provided valuable insights into the various triggers, consequences, and recovery trajectories, offering a reservoir of knowledge for crafting resilient investment strategies.

Chapter 4: Digital Assets in Downturns

Transitioning into Chapter 4, we explored the contemporary landscape of digital assets and their role as alternative investments during economic challenges. The emergence of digital art and other assets marked a paradigm shift, illustrating the importance of diversification and adaptability in navigating evolving markets. As we reflect on this chapter, the theme of embracing innovation and recognizing new investment opportunities stands out.

Synthesizing Foundations

As we synthesize the insights from Chapters 1 to 4, a clear narrative emerges. Resilient investing requires a multifaceted approach that begins with a foundational understanding of economic cycles, the historical context of recessions, and an openness to innovative investment opportunities. Preparedness, adaptability, and a proactive mindset serve as the cornerstones for navigating turbulent times. This sets the stage for the next segment, where we delve into strategies and actions that investors can undertake during recessions.

Chapter 5: Market Behavior During Recessions

In Chapter 5, we delved into the intricate dance of financial markets during recessions. Understanding how markets typically respond in downturns is crucial for making informed decisions. We explored the dynamics of fear and greed, emphasizing the importance of a level-headed approach amidst market fluctuations. The insights from this chapter form a bridge to the subsequent discussions on emotional resilience and proactive investment strategies.

Chapter 6: Emotional Resilience in Investing

Chapter 6 took a deep dive into the emotional rollercoaster that accompanies market turbulence. Managing emotions and avoiding panic emerged as essential skills for investors. By recognizing the psychological factors that influence decision-making, readers gained tools to navigate the emotional terrain of investing. As we reflect on this chapter, the theme of maintaining composure and rationality in the face of uncertainty resonates.

Chapter 7: Investment Strategies During Recessions

Building on the emotional resilience discussed in Chapter 6, Chapter 7 provided a roadmap for proactive investment strategies during recessions. From value investing to tactical asset allocation, readers were equipped with a toolkit to tailor their approaches based on market conditions. This chapter emphasized the importance of staying nimble, adapting strategies to changing landscapes, and seizing opportunities amid adversity.

Chapter 8: Risk Management

Chapter 8 underscored the critical role of risk management in the investment process. Understanding and mitigating risks became paramount, aligning with the overarching theme of resilience. By implementing effective risk management strategies, investors can protect their portfolios and enhance their ability to navigate economic downturns with confidence.

Synthesizing Proactive Strategies

As we synthesize the insights from Chapters 5 to 8, a coherent narrative emerges. Proactive strategies during recessions involve a dynamic interplay between understanding market behavior, cultivating emotional resilience, and deploying a diversified set of investment strategies. From tactical asset allocation to robust risk management, the ability to adapt and act decisively is fundamental to thriving in uncertain times. This sets the stage for the final segment, where we explore expert perspectives and lessons that transcend market cycles.

Chapter 9: Case Studies - Successful Investments

Chapter 9 offered real-life examples of successful investments during recessions. By examining case studies, readers gained insights into the strategies employed by savvy investors who not only weathered economic storms but emerged stronger. These stories serve as beacons of inspiration, illustrating the application of diverse approaches and reinforcing the notion that opportunities abound even in challenging times.

Chapter 10: Preparing for the Aftermath

In Chapter 10, we shifted our focus to preparing for the aftermath of recessions. By identifying post-recession opportunities, understanding economic recovery patterns, and exploring sectors poised for growth, readers were equipped with a forward-looking mindset. This chapter laid the groundwork for the subsequent discussions on sustainable investing, technological innovations, and global perspectives.

Chapter 11: Expert Insights

Chapter 11 served as a repository of wisdom from seasoned investors, financial advisors, institutional investors, economic analysts, and technological innovators. By gathering diverse perspectives, readers gained a panoramic view of expert insights spanning the realms of value investing, technological advancements, sustainable practices, and risk management. This chapter offered a comprehensive tapestry of wisdom that informs the final reflections on navigating uncertainty.

Synthesizing Expert Perspectives and Future Outlook

As we synthesize the insights from Chapters 9 to 11, a tapestry of expert perspectives unfolds. Successful investments are not limited to a specific strategy but rather emanate from a combination of resilience, adaptability, and a keen understanding of market dynamics. Expert insights provide a compass for readers to navigate the complexities of investing, offering a nuanced approach that transcends traditional boundaries. This sets the stage for the concluding segment, where we encapsulate the key takeaways and encourage readers to embark on their own journey of thriving in uncertain times.

Conclusion: A Roadmap for Resilient Investing

Parting Thoughts

As we conclude this exploration of thriving through turbulence, the tapestry woven from Chapters 1 to 11 forms a roadmap for resilient investing. From understanding the foundations of economic cycles to deploying proactive strategies during recessions and embracing expert perspectives, readers are equipped with a holistic framework.

Key Takeaways

The journey through these chapters has imparted several key takeaways:

Preparedness and Understanding: A foundation of preparedness, grounded in a deep understanding of economic cycles and historical contexts, is essential for resilient investing.

Adaptability and Emotional Resilience: Navigating market uncertainties requires adaptability and emotional resilience. The ability to stay composed during market fluctuations is as crucial as the strategies themselves.

Proactive Strategies: Proactive investment strategies involve a dynamic interplay between market behavior analysis, emotional resilience, and a diversified approach to risk management. The toolkit includes value investing, tactical asset allocation, and robust risk management practices.

Expert Perspectives: Learning from seasoned investors, financial advisors, institutional investors, and technological innovators provides a wealth of insights that transcend market cycles. Expert perspectives serve as guideposts for navigating the complexities of the investment landscape.

Forward-Looking Mindset: Looking beyond recessions, identifying post-recession opportunities, and aligning investment strategies with future trends are essential components of a forward-looking mindset.

Encouraging Resilient Action

As readers embark on their own investment journeys, the call to action is clear. Embrace the wisdom gained from these chapters, continuously adapt to evolving market dynamics and approach uncertainties with a proactive and informed mindset. Resilient investing is not a destination but an ongoing journey, and by synthesizing the lessons learned, readers can navigate the ever-changing seas of the global economy with confidence.

This concluding chapter is an invitation for readers to leverage the insights gained and embark on their own roadmap for resilient investing. As we part ways, the journey of thriving through turbulence continues, guided by the principles of preparedness, adaptability, and a forward-looking mindset.

www.ingramcontent.com/pod-product-compliance
Lightning Source LLC
LaVergne TN
LVHW090418210926
848480LV00002B/613
9798224477678